Globalization: A Very Short Introduction

Very Short Introductions available now:

Available soon:

For more information visit our website

www.oup.com/vsi/

Manfred B. Steger

GLOBALIZATION

A Very Short Introduction

FIFTH EDITION

OXFORD
UNIVERSITY PRESS

Great Clarendon Street, Oxford, OX2 6DP,
United Kingdom

Oxford University Press is a department of the University of Oxford.
It furthers the University's objective of excellence in research, scholarship,
and education by publishing worldwide. Oxford is a registered trade mark of
Oxford University Press in the UK and in certain other countries

© Manfred B. Steger 2020

The moral rights of the author have been asserted

First edition published 2003
Second edition published 2009
Third edition published 2013
Fourth edition published 2017
This edition published 2020

Impression: 3

Published in the United States of America by Oxford University Press
198 Madison Avenue, New York, NY 10016, United States of America

British Library Cataloguing in Publication Data

Data available

Library of Congress Control Number: 2019957384

ISBN 978-0-19-884945-2

Printed in Great Britain by
Ashford Colour Press Ltd, Gosport, Hampshire

Links to third party websites are provided by Oxford in good faith and
for information only. Oxford disclaims any responsibility for the materials
contained in any third party website referenced in this work.

*For Emmet, Milo, Shunie, Skaya, Yolanda,
and all the other children born in this
century who face a difficult global future*

Contents

Contents

List of illustrations

List of maps

Reproduced with permission from De Backer, K. and S. Miroudot (2013), 'Mapping Global Value Chains', OECD Trade Policy Papers, No. 159, OECD Publishing, Paris, <https://doi.org/10.1787/5k3v1trgnbr4-en>

Source: based on information from UNOCHA.org

Ssolbergj / Wikimedia (CC BY-SA 3.0)

List of figures

List of abbreviations

APEC	Asian Pacific Economic Cooperation
ASEAN	Association of Southeast Asian Nations
BWR	Bretton Woods regime
BCE	Before the Common Era
CE	Common Era
CEO	chief executive officer
CFCs	chlorofluorocarbons
CITES	Convention on International Trade in Endangered Species of Wild Flora and Fauna
ECB	European Central Bank
ESDC	European Sovereign Debt Crisis
EU	European Union
FDI	Foreign Direct Investment
G20	Group of Twenty
GATT	General Agreement on Tariffs and Trade
GDP	gross domestic product
GFC	Global Financial Crisis
GJM	Global Justice Movement
GPS	Global Positioning System
ICT	information and communications technology
IMF	International Monetary Fund
INGO	international non-governmental organization
ISIS	Islamic State of Iraq and Syria (and Levant)

MERCOSUR	Mercado Común del Sur (Southern Common Market)
MSF/DWB	Médecins Sans Frontières/Doctors Without Borders
NAFTA	North American Free Trade Agreement
NATO	North Atlantic Treaty Organization
NGO	non-governmental organization
NYC	New York City
OAU	Organization of African Unity
OECD	Organization for Economic Cooperation and Development
OLED TV	Organic Light Emitting Diode Television
OPEC	Organization of Petroleum Exporting Countries
OWS	Occupy Wall Street
SAPs	Structural Adjustment Programmes
TNCs	transnational corporations
TPP	Trans-Pacific Partnership
UK	United Kingdom
UN	United Nations
UNCTAD	United Nations Conference on Trade and Development
UNESCO	United Nations Educational, Scientific, and Cultural Organization
UNIPCC	United Nations Intergovernmental Panel on Climate Change
US	United States (of America)
WC	Washington Consensus
WEF	World Economic Forum
WHO	World Health Organization
WSF	World Social Forum

Preface to the fifth edition

It is a gratifying experience to present readers with the fifth edition of a short book that has been so well received—not only in the English-speaking world, but around the world in more than twenty languages. The necessary task of updating and expanding it has not been easy in light of proliferating global problems such as social inequality, climate change, cyber-insecurity, mass migration, civil wars, trade wars, automation, new pandemics, and the unexpected surge of national populism around the world. Indeed, President Trump's challenge to the postwar international order and the growing influence of contending powers such as China, India, and Russia has leading experts wondering whether we find ourselves at the beginning of a new age of deglobalization.

Keeping such a complex topic as globalization both brief and accessible in such unsettled times becomes even more challenging in the case of a *very short* introduction. For this reason, the authors of the few existing brief introductions to the subject tend to concentrate on only one or two aspects of globalization—usually the emergence of the high-tech global economy, its history, structure, and supposed benefits and shortcomings. To be sure, this single focus is helpful in explaining the impact and consequences of new techno-economic networks connecting people across borders and the transnational flows of goods, services, and labour. At the same time, such narrow accounts often leave the reader with a limited understanding of the full complexity of globalization.

The transformative powers of global interdependence reach deeply into *all* aspects of contemporary social life. Hence, the present volume makes the case that globalization also contains important *cultural* and *ideological* aspects in the form of politically charged meanings and stories that describe and define that very process. The political forces behind these competing accounts utilize the transnational media to endow the buzzword with norms, values, and understandings that not only legitimize and advance their specific power interests, but also shape the personal and collective identities of billions of people. After all, it is mostly the *normative* question of whether globalization ought to be considered a 'good' or a 'bad' thing that has spawned heated debates in classrooms, boardrooms, and on the streets.

Some commentators applaud globalization for its proven ability to lift millions of people out of poverty and provide instant communication and almost limitless access to information. Nowhere has the success of economic globalization been more visible than in the impressive rise of Asian societies. Others condemn globalization as a destructive force that annihilates traditional communal values, wrecks our planet, and stretches social disparities beyond sustainable levels. Paradoxically, both sides draw on reams of 'empirical data' to bolster their respective views. Regardless of which position is favoured, readers would be well advised to maintain a *critical* stance towards both interpretations.

On the whole, I am well disposed toward globalization. I believe that we should take comfort in the fact that the world is becoming a more interdependent place with the potential of enhancing people's lives. Surely, enhancing people's mobility and connecting them across political borders and cultural divides represents an exciting development. I also welcome sensible and humane policies that allow for the global flow of migrants and refugees. The same goes for technological progress, as long as it remains accountable to autonomous citizens rather than reducing them to the status of exploitable 'users'. In a nutshell, globalization must go hand in hand with the betterment of *all* people, especially those living in the disadvantaged regions of the global South. Most importantly, securing sustainable forms of globalization demands that we take better care of our beautiful planet.

Today, the study of globalization extends beyond any single academic discipline. Yet, its lack of a firm disciplinary home also contains opportunities. *Global Studies* has emerged as a popular new field of academic enquiry organized around four major conceptual pillars: globalization, transdisciplinarity, space and time, and critical thinking. Hundreds of Global Studies programmes have been established on all continents, inviting thousands of students to study globalization across traditional disciplinary boundaries in the social sciences, humanities, and even the natural sciences. The surging transdisciplinary field covers vast literatures on related subjects that are usually studied in isolation from each other. The greatest challenge facing Global Studies lies, therefore, in synthesizing the various strands of knowledge in a way that does justice to the increasingly fluid and interdependent nature of our fast-changing world.

Let me end this Preface by recording my debts of gratitude. First, I want to thank my colleagues and students at the University of Hawai'i-Mānoa and Western Sydney University. Special thanks are due to Paul James, the Director of the Institute for Culture and Society at Western Sydney University, for his steady intellectual encouragement and deep friendship. Second, I appreciate the helpful feedback from colleagues from around the world who share my enthusiasm for the study of globalization. Third, I want to express my sincere appreciation to numerous readers, reviewers, and audiences around the world, who, for more than two decades, have made insightful comments in response to my public lectures and publications on the subject.

Dr Franz Broswimmer, a dear friend and innovative environmentalist, deserves special recognition for his continuing supply of valuable information on the ecological aspects of globalization. I especially appreciate Dr Tommaso Durante's competent research assistance on this edition as well as his formidable artist's eye for choosing suitable illustrations. Tommaso's pioneering 'Visual Archive Project of the Global Imaginary' can be found at: <http://www.the-visual-archive-project-of-the-global-imaginary.com/>.

Andrea Keegan and Jenny Nugee, my editors at Oxford University Press, have been shining examples of professionalism. Finally, I want to thank my wife Perle Besserman—as well as the Steger and Besserman-Trigère families—for their love and support. Many people have contributed to improving the quality of this book; its remaining flaws are my own responsibility.

Chapter 1
What is globalization?

The earliest appearance of the term 'globalization' in the English language can be traced back to the 1930s. But it was not until the 1990s that the concept took the world by storm. The new buzzword captured the increasingly interconnected nature of social life on our planet and foregrounded the global integration of markets turbocharged by the ICT revolution. Three decades on, globalization has remained a hot topic that has recently been subjected to growing criticism—especially from the resurgent national populist forces around the world. Today, one can track millions of references to the term in both virtual and printed spaces that range from enthusiastic embrace to blanket condemnation.

But 'globalization' has also been variably used in both the popular press and academic literature to describe a process, a condition, a system, a force, and an age. Given that these concepts have very different meanings, their indiscriminate usage is often obscure and invites confusion. For example, a sloppy conflation of process and condition encourages circular definitions that explain little. The often-repeated truism that globalization (the process?) leads to more globalization (the condition?) does not allow us to draw meaningful analytical distinctions between causes and effects.

Three key concepts: *globality, global imaginary, globalization*

To sharpen our initial understanding of the subject, let us distinguish between three different, but related, concepts. First, *globality* signifies a *social condition* characterized by tight global economic, political, cultural, and environmental interconnections and flows that challenges most of the currently existing borders and boundaries. Yet, we should not assume that globality is already upon us—it's a possible future condition. Nor does the term suggest a determinate endpoint that precludes any further development. In fact, we could easily imagine different social manifestations of globality: one might be based primarily on values of individualism, competition, and laissez-faire capitalism, while another might draw on more communal norms and cooperative values.

Second, *global imaginary* refers to people's growing *consciousness* of the world as a single whole. This does not mean that national and local frameworks have lost their power to provide people with a sense of home and identity. But it would be a mistake to close one's eyes to the weakening of the national imaginary, as it has been historically constructed in the 19th and 20th centuries. The intensification of global consciousness destabilizes and unsettles the nation-state framework within which people imagine their communal existence. As we shall see in Chapter 7, the rising global imaginary is also powerfully reflected in the current transformation of political ideologies and the social values that go into the articulation of concrete policy agendas and programmes.

Our final and major key term, *globalization*, is a spatial concept signifying a *matrix of social processes* that is transforming our present social condition of conventional nationality into one of globality. Like 'modernization' and other verbal nouns that end in the suffix '-ization', the concept suggests an evolving dynamism along discernible patterns. Such unfolding may occur quickly or slowly, but it always indicates social change. As global studies scholar Roland Benedikter puts it, we are in the midst of a 'global systemic shift'.

But what sort of 'systemic shift' is being named by 'globalization'? The root term 'global' seems to indicate processes that operate exclusively at the transnational level such as the operation of global markets, worldwide investment flows, or the establishment of institutions of global reach such as the International Criminal Court based in the Netherlands. However, as Global Studies scholar Saskia Sassen emphasizes, there is another set of globalizing processes that is not confined to the scale of the 'global'. Rather, it takes place deep inside the 'regional', 'national', and 'local' domains. Rather than becoming extinct or irrelevant, these subglobal spaces get entangled with the global to produce multi-spatial forms of human contact. Global Studies scholars refer to this complex interplay between the global and the local/national as *glocalization*. In short, globalization is really glocalization.

But many people still have trouble recognizing that globalization affects all geographical scales ranging from the local to the global. If we asked ordinary persons on the busy streets of global cities like New York, London, Shanghai, São Paulo, or Sydney about the essence of globalization, their answers would probably involve some reference to growing forms of global connectivity fuelled by digital technologies. They might point to their mobile devices such as Cloud-connected smart wireless phones like the Android or sleek digital tablets like the iPad linked to powerful Internet browsers like Google Chrome that sort in a split second through gigantic data sets. Or they might mention the burgeoning video-postings on YouTube; ubiquitous social networking sites like Facebook and Twitter; the blogosphere; Cloud-based voice services like Amazon's Alexa; satellite- and computer-connected OLED TVs, Netflix movie streaming; interactive 3-D computer and video games; and the new generation of voice-activated GPS and navigation units soon to be installed in self-driving cars.

Although digital technology is only a part of the larger phenomenon we call 'globalization', it would be foolish to deny that these technological innovations have played a crucial role in the current compression of world-time and world-space. The Internet (see Figure A), in particular, has assumed a pivotal function in the expanding global–local nexus. After all, the World Wide Web connects billions of individuals, thousands of civil society

A. What happens in an Internet minute in 2019?

associations, and hundreds of governments located at specific places on our planet.

Thus, it makes sense to start our exploratory journey into the heart of globalization with a concrete example that highlights the awesome glocal impact of digital technology on 21st-century societies. Let us turn to the amazing, yet true, story of a young American journalist whose loss of his cell phone gained him millions of fans in China and around the world.

How a stolen iPhone made a young American a Chinese Internet celebrity

After a Happy Hour wine binge in an NYC East Village bar in February 2014, Matt Stopera noticed that his iPhone was missing. As a young American journalist working for Buzzfeed—a US-based Internet news and entertainment company with a focus on digital media—the loss of his cell phone was almost tantamount to losing his eyesight. After recovering from his initial shock, Matt did what the millions of global victims of cell phone theft tend to do: he got a new one and tried to forget the frustrating experience as quickly as possible. Most cell phone theft stories end here. But Matt's didn't.

A year later, he was sitting in his small flat in NYC browsing through his private photo stream on his new cell phone when he came across a slew of pictures he had not taken. They included more than twenty images of a young Asian man standing in front of an orange tree. For over a month, daily updates of the 'orange man' pictures kept popping up on Matt's new phone. Trying to solve the mystery, he consulted with an Apple Genius employee who speculated that his lost iPhone was most likely somewhere in China. That's where most stolen cell phones end up—millions each year. The Apple genius also revealed the reason for the appearance of these alien pictures: his current phone and the stolen one were still sharing the same iCloud account. Matt immediately deleted everything on his phone and asked for his former device to be deactivated. Confident that these actions would put an end to the hassle, he left the Apple store.

On second thought, however, Matt decided to get to the bottom of the mystery. To that end, he created a post on BuzzFeed: *Who is this man and why are his pictures showing up on my phone?* Within hours, he received numerous tweets from Chinese people offering him help in finding 'orange man'. But how could there be such a swift and massive response from hundreds of tweeters thousands of miles away? In fact, a famous user of Sina Weibo—a Chinese micro-blogging website and leading social media platform with over 400 million monthly active users—had cross-posted his BuzzFeed post, thus triggering the virtual hunt for the mystery 'orange man' that soon went viral. Told that he had become an overnight Internet celebrity in China, Matt followed the advice of his new virtual fans and joined Weibo. The next day, he had 50,000 followers. Within a week, the number climbed to 160,000. Soon thereafter, he broke through the 1,000,000 barrier.

By that time, the mystery man, Li Hongjun, had been found in the south-east coastal province of Guandong. Paying close attention to this viral explosion, Weibo gave Li the nickname 'Brother Orange' and encouraged the two men to meet in China. Within days, the story skyrocketed to the top of Weibo's trending topics as 60 million users were following along to see if and when the pair would meet. Many of them began signing up for US-based social networking platforms like Facebook and Twitter, even though these sites were technically banned in China. Matt also responded to numerous requests from his Chinese fans to start teaching them English using video posts. As this tutoring venture took off, he received the Chinese nickname 'Doubi', which translates loosely as 'Mr Bean'. At this point, 'Doubi' and 'Bro' Orange' had been exchanging electronic messages on a daily basis. The enhanced frequency of their interactions revealed more about their

respective backgrounds and life-stories. It revealed that Bro'
Orange was a married man with four children and owned a
successful restaurant called Jade Tea Farm in Meizhou, a thriving
city of 4.3 million.

In March 2015, their highly anticipated meeting took place. On
Matt's three-legged plane flight from NYC to Guandong, he was
recognized and mobbed by several Chinese passengers. Upon
landing at Meizhou airport, Matt was greeted by droves of fans
who had queued up for hours to welcome their American idol.
As Matt put it, 'Basically, I now know what it feels like to be Kim K
at LAX with Kanye and Northwest.' Wildly cheering the first
hug between the two long-distance iPhoto pals, the fans also
applauded the return of the stolen iPhone to its original owner.
It turned out that Li was entirely innocent, having received the
phone as a gift from a distant relative.

Talking through translators, and sponsored by Weibo, the pair
embarked on a triumphant publicity tour through Li's home
province. Their lavish means of transport included a comfortable
bus and two special cars that featured big decals of their faces as
well as Mandarin characters and English words advertising the
tour. Their journey was heavily documented on social media and
included a symbolic signing ceremony of a 'Chinese–American
friendship treaty' between the two correspondents who were
quickly becoming close friends. Followed every minute by a large
press contingent demanding constant interviews, the pair
interacted with numerous local fans, who held up gigantic
welcome signs and were eager to take selfies with their heroes.
The publicity tour included many happenings designed to
showcase Chinese culture, first by costuming Matt in the clothes
of a traditional Chinese girl before setting out on a tour including
public tastings of famous Chinese dishes; inspections of large
rural tea farms and recently founded wineries; performances of
old Chinese folk songs; and even a visit to a local Communist
leader's memorial shrine.

1. Buzzfeed writer Matt 'Doubi' Stopera and Li 'Brother Orange' Hongjun visit Beijing's Tiananmen Square.

The pair's week-long journey ended with a memorable Weibo-sponsored trip to Beijing, where they visited famous landmarks like Tiananmen Square (Figure 1). Trailed by a growing media entourage and the now familiar throngs of fans, the men found it difficult to escape public attention. Even China's largest TV station, CCTV News, got in on the act and dedicated several minutes of primetime national coverage to their visit to the capital.

After Matt's trip to China, Li returned the favour and paid a highly advertised visit to his American pal. Matt showed off his NYC home turf and also took his Bro' to Las Vegas. Unexpectedly, the celebrity pair was invited to NBC's Emmy Award-winning *The Ellen DeGeneres Show*. Eager to introduce the odd couple to a larger American audience, the famous host jokingly referred to herself as 'Sister Orange' and encouraged American and Chinese followers to exchange messages. Enjoying their superstar status, the pair also attended a Britney Spears concert where they met the pop diva in private session and took loads of pictures that delighted the fans back in China.

Eventually, the astonishing story of how a stolen iPhone made an ordinary American a Chinese Internet celebrity was shared internationally on social media more than 100 million times. And it continued on the same implausible trajectory that it had started out on in 2014. The Hollywood entertainment giant Warner Brothers announced in 2016 that it would co-produce *Brother Orange* for the big screen, with TV sitcom *Big Bang Theory* lead Jim Parsons playing Matt Stopera and noted Chinese actor Dong Chengpeng starring as Li Hongjun. Although the development of the movie proceeded slowly, the project is still alive and slated to begin shooting in 2020.

What the stolen iPhone story can tell us about the forms, qualities, and dimensions of globalization

The remarkable story of Matt Stopera's stolen iPhone not only makes for fantastic entertainment, but also yields important insights into the complex dynamics of globalization. First, as we noted at the outset of this chapter, the tale demonstrates that the local and global should not be seen as opposites. Rather, they constitute interrelated nodes of expanding social interconnections encompassing all spatial scales. This intensifying local–global nexus was reflected in many ways during Matt's visit to China. Consider, for example, the pictures of him dressed up in traditional Guandong girl's clothing, which were instantly shared on global social media platforms. Or think of Chinese fans welcoming the pair to their local towns and villages holding up hand-painted welcome signs that also featured globally recognizable QR codes. These matrix barcodes are now utilized by millions of individuals and businesses to store commercial information as well as to advertise products and services globally

Box 1. Glocalization in action: the magic of QR codes

'QR' stands for 'quick response' and refers to those square-shaped, black-and-white barcodes made up of hundreds of shapes of 'bits' that nowadays adorn most products and advertisements. By using a cell phone and a QR readers app, scanning a QR code might yield the price of the product, make a payment, track a shipment, identify documents, display a text, connect to a wireless network, or open a webpage in the cell phone's browser. Or, as was the case with the QR code placed on handmade signs welcoming Matt and Li to cities and villages in Guandong province, it might yield a globally accessible website advertising the local event. Invented in 1994 by the Japanese company Denso Wave to track vehicles, the largest QR codes can store up to 15,000 bits that can be arranged in 2.81796087 $9631397637428637785383222308241674912977296 \times 10^{4515}$ different ways—a number larger than all traceable items on Earth combined.

(see Box 1). Or consider the making of *Brother Orange*, a major feature film intended for global distribution. The venture united four production companies located at specific sites around the world under the commercial umbrella of a transnational enterprise called 'Flagship Entertainment': American-based Warner Brothers and BuzzFeed Studios, China-based China Media Capital, and Hong Kong-based broadcaster TVB.

Another important insight emerging from our stolen cell phone story suggests that globalization should not be seen as a monolithic social process. Rather, it assumes several distinct, but interrelated, *social forms* that contain a number of different qualities or characteristics. We can identify at least four major forms of globalization that overlay each other in complex patterns of practice and meaning.

The first social form, *embodied globalization*, involves the movement of people across our planet. As we shall discuss in Chapters 2 and 3, this is the oldest form of globalization and remains enduringly relevant in the contemporary movement of refugees, migrants, travellers, entrepreneurs, temporary workers, tourists, and so on (see Box 2). Concrete 21st-century examples include African political refugees crossing the Mediterranean into Europe and Central American migrants trying to trek across the Rio Grande valley into the United States in search of more sustainable lives. Matt Stopera, the young protagonist of our iPhone story, embodied globalization as a privileged tourist who completed the 7,894-mile trip from NYC to Meizhou in less than twenty-four hours in the comfort and security of an aeroplane cabin. Only a century ago, the same journey would have taken several gruelling weeks spent on ships, trains, motorcars, and horse- or oxen-drawn carriages, forcing the traveller to make his way to China in much less luxurious and safe circumstances.

The second form, *disembodied globalization*, is characterized by the extension of social relations through the movement of immaterial things and processes, including words, images, and electronic texts, and encoded capital such as crypto-currencies like Bitcoin. As demonstrated by Matt's story 'going viral' on global

Box 2. Embodied globalization: where on Earth do you want go?

Travel has never been more popular. Last year there were 1.4 billion overseas arrivals throughout the world. The total number of international and domestic trips taken is a staggering 7 billion! And experts predict an increase to 8 billion by 2022. Travel is the second fastest growing industry worldwide; manufacturing is still slightly ahead. In 2018, travel injected a whopping US$12.33 trillion into the global economy.

social media platforms, this form has taken an enormous qualitative leap with the digital revolution. In fact, disembodied globalization is emerging as the dominant dynamic of the 21st century. The latest available data on digital global flows show that the amount of cross-border bandwidth in 2016 has grown to be forty-five times larger than in 2005, making the world more digitally connected than ever. Thus, commentators have heralded a 'new era of *digital globalization*', an observation which seems powerfully confirmed by the 100 million electronic shares of the Brother Orange story.

The third form, *object-extended globalization*, refers to the global movement of objects—in particular traded commodities—as well as those ubiquitous early objects of financial exchange such as shells, coins, and notes. It takes us from the goods travelling on the ancient Silk Road from China to the Roman Empire to the development of modern shipping containers crossing the world's oceans. Moreover, it includes the digitally controlled delivery system of Amazon.com that will offer drone-operated services in the near future as well as traded global commodities like Matt's stolen iPhone making its illegal way to China; pre-loved pairs of Levi's jeans produced in the sweatshops of Bangladesh and destined for the coolest fashion temples of Milan; and the relics and treasures of antiquity sold at skyrocketing prices at international Internet auctions.

The fourth and final form, *organization-extended globalization*, corresponds to the global extension of social and political institutions such as empires, states, corporations, NGOs, clubs, and so on. Its history can be traced back at least as far as the expansionist empires of Egypt, Persia, China, and Rome, and the proselytizing of the agents of Christendom more than a millennium ago. More recent examples include the half-million US military personnel stationed around the world, the global franchises of fast food enterprises like Subway or KFC; and China's mind-boggling 'One Belt One Road' initiative—a monumental infrastructure project designed to extend Chinese economic and political influence across Asia and deep into Europe. As reflected in Matt's amazing adventure, other examples of organization-extended globalization include Weibo's successful organization of his China visit (as well as Li's America visit); the transnational promotion of 'traditional' Chinese cultural institutions; and Warner Brothers' ability to reach across the Pacific to find eager co-producers for their *Brother Orange* venture.

Indeed, all four forms of globalization are on clear display in our stolen iPhone tale. Moreover, they possess distinct qualities or characteristics. First, they involve both the *creation* of new social networks and the *multiplication* of existing connections that cut across traditional political, economic, cultural, and geographical boundaries. As Matt's publicity events in China demonstrate, today's media combine conventional TV coverage with multiple streaming feeds into digital devices and social networking sites that transcend nationally based services.

A second quality inherent in these four principal forms of globalization is the *expansion* or *stretching* of social relations, activities, and connections. Today's financial markets reach around the globe, and electronic trading occurs around the clock. Gigantic and virtually identical shopping malls have emerged across the globe, catering to those consumers who can afford commodities from all regions of the world—including products whose various components were manufactured in different countries. This process of social stretching applies to commercial enterprises like Warner Brothers eager to make money off Matt and Li's experiences; non-governmental organizations dedicated to aiding people living in poverty; exclusive social clubs frequented by the wealthy 1 per cent; and countless regional and global institutions and associations: the UN, the EU, ASEAN, APEC, the OAU, MERCOSUR, and the WEF, to name but a few.

Third, all forms of globalization also involve the *intensification* and *acceleration* of social exchanges and activities. As the Spanish sociologist Manuel Castells has pointed out, we have witnessed the creation of a *global network society* fuelled by what he calls *communication power*. As demonstrated in our tale of Brother Orange, this new form of power draws its strength from technological innovations that are reshaping the social landscape of human life.

Fourth, globalization does not merely unfold on an objective, material level but also involves the *subjective* plane of *human consciousness*. Without erasing local and national attachments, the compression of the world into a single place has increasingly made the whole planet the frame of reference for human thought and action. In other words, globalization involves both the macro-structures of a global community and the micro-structures of global personhood. Mediated by digital technology controlled by large TNCs that mine human experience for commercial profit, the global extends deep into the core of the personal self and its dispositions and facilitates the creation of multiple individual and collective identities like 'Bro' Orange', 'Doubi', or the Manchester United football fan club.

Finally, these *four forms* and *four qualities of globalization* infuse simultaneously the major social dimensions of everyday life: economics, politics, culture, ideology, and so on. Yet, globalization has often been analysed and explained by various commentators in a rather one-dimensional manner. The ancient Buddhist parable of the blind scholars and their encounter with the elephant helps to illustrate the academic controversy over the significance of various dimensions of globalization. Since the blind scholars did not know what the elephant looked like, they resolved to obtain a mental picture, and thus the knowledge they desired, by touching the animal. Feeling its trunk, one blind man argued that the elephant was like a gigantic snake. Another man, rubbing along its enormous leg, likened the animal to a rough column of

2. The globalization scholars and the elephant.

massive proportions. The third person took hold of its tail and insisted that the elephant resembled a large, flexible brush. The fourth man felt its sharp tusks and declared it to be like a great spear. Each of the blind scholars held firmly to his own idea of what constituted an elephant. Since their scholarly reputation was riding on the veracity of their respective findings, the blind men never ceased arguing over the true nature of the elephant (see Figure 2).

The academic quarrel over which dimension contains the essence of globalization represents a postmodern version of the parable of the blind men and the elephant. Global Studies scholars who equate globalization with a singular process clash with others over which aspect of social life constitutes its primary domain. Many experts argue that economic processes lie at the core of globalization. Others privilege political, cultural, or ideological aspects. Still others point to environmental processes as being the essence of globalization. Like the blind men in the parable, each globalization researcher is partly right by correctly identifying *one* important dimension of the phenomenon in question. However, their collective mistake lies in their dogmatic attempts to reduce

15

such a complex phenomenon as globalization to one or two domains that correspond to their own expertise.

To make matters even more complex, globalization is a geographically uneven process that not only connects but sometimes also disrupts existing relations. This means that people living in various parts of the world are affected very differently by this gigantic compression of space and time. Unsurprisingly, then, scholars not only hold different views with regard to primary dimensions of globalization, they also disagree on its scale, causation, chronology, impact, trajectories, and policy outcomes. For this reason, they have raised a myriad research questions that run in all directions. How does globalization proceed? What is driving it? Does it have one cause or is there a combination of factors? Is globalization a continuation of modernity or is it a radical break? Does it create new forms of inequality and hierarchy? Notice that whenever researchers try to bring their object of enquiry into sharper focus, they also heighten the danger of provoking scholarly disagreements. Our subject is no exception.

Towards a *very short* definition of globalization

Fortunately, our examination of the forms, qualities, and dimensions of globalization reflected in our stolen iPhone story have prepared us to tackle the academic task of assembling a digestible working definition of a contested concept that has proven notoriously hard to pin down. Surely, a central task for the new field of Global Studies must be to devise sophisticated yet accessible ways for gauging the relative importance of each dimension of globalization without losing sight of the whole phenomenon. Despite the existing differences of opinion on the subject, it should be possible to come up with a *general definition* that satisfies most experts. Drawing on the insights that have emerged from our discussion, let us close this chapter by compressing our initial findings into a single sentence that yields the following *short definition* of globalization in seventeen words:

Globalization refers to the multidimensional and uneven intensification of social relations and consciousness across world-time and world-space.

Given the subtitle of our book, however, we ought to do even better by cutting our word count even further. So here is a *very short* definition of globalization in six words:

Globalization is about intensifying planetary interconnectivity.

Chapter 2
Globalization in history

In this chapter, we consider an important objection raised by Global Studies scholars sensitive to historical matters: is globalization really a new phenomenon that is fundamentally different from the centuries-old process of modernization? Some critics have responded to this question in the negative, contending that even a cursory look at history suggests that there is not much that is new about contemporary globalization. Hence, before we explore in some detail the major dimensions of globalization, we should give this argument a fair hearing. After all, a critical investigation of globalization's alleged novelty and its relationship to modernity is closely related to yet another question hotly debated by globalization experts: what would a proper historical chronology and periodization of globalization look like?

The *short definition* of globalization we arrived at in Chapter 1 stresses its dynamic and multidimensional nature. In fact, the spatial expansion of social relations and the corresponding rise of the global imaginary are gradual processes with deep historical roots. The computer and software engineers who developed Matt's iPhone or the self-driving cars of the future stand on the shoulders of earlier innovators who created the steam engine, the cotton gin, the telegraph, the phonograph, the telephone, the typewriter, the internal-combustion engine, and electrical appliances. These products, in turn, owe their existence to much earlier technological inventions such as the telescope, the compass, water wheels, windmills, gunpowder, the printing press, and oceangoing ships. And these innovations were the collective achievement of humans in all regions of the world, not just in one privileged geographic 'centre' called the 'West' or the 'North'. In order to acknowledge the full historical record of growing interdependence, we might reach back even further to such momentous technological and social achievements as the production of paper, the development of writing, the invention of the wheel, the domestication of wild plants and animals, the slow outward migration of our common African ancestors, and, finally, the emergence of language and the taming of fire at the dawn of human evolution.

Thus, the answer to the question of whether globalization constitutes a new phenomenon depends upon how far we are willing to extend the web of causation that resulted in those recent technologies and social arrangements that most people have come to associate with our buzzword. Some Global Studies scholars consciously limit the historical scope of globalization to the post-1989 era in order to capture the uniqueness of its contemporary speed. Others are willing to extend this timeframe to include the groundbreaking developments of the last two centuries since the Industrial Revolution. Still others argue that globalization really represents the continuation and extension of complex processes that began with the emergence of modernity and the capitalist world system in the 1500s. And the remaining researchers refuse to confine globalization to time periods measured in mere decades or centuries. Rather, they suggest that these processes have been unfolding for millennia.

No doubt, each of these contending perspectives contains important insights. As we will see in this book, the advocates of the first approach have marshalled impressive evidence for their view that the dramatic expansion and acceleration of global exchanges since the 1980s represents a big leap in the history of globalization. The proponents of the second view correctly emphasize the tight connection between contemporary forms of globalization and the explosion of technology known as the Industrial Revolution. The representatives of the third perspective rightly point to the significance of the time–space compression that occurred in the 16th century when Eurasia, Africa, and the Americas first became connected by enduring trade routes. Finally, the advocates of the fourth approach advance a rather sensible argument when they insist that any truly comprehensive account of globalization falls short without the incorporation of ancient developments and long-term dynamics into our planetary history.

While my short chronology of globalization that frames this chapter is necessarily fragmentary and general, it identifies five historical periods that are separated from each other by significant shifts in the pace of social exchanges as well as a widening of geographical scope. Thus, we could say that globalization is an ancient process that, over many centuries, has crossed distinct qualitative thresholds. Like a car transmission that accelerates the speed of the car, globalization has been shifting into higher gears while also taking some steps back at times. But let me reiterate that my chronology does not advocate a Eurocentric perspective of world history. Involving all major regions and cultures of our planet, global history has unfolded in multidirectional flows originating from multiple civilizational centres. Moreover, the history of globalization is not a steady, linear ascent, but a constant up and down full of unanticipated surprises, violent twists, and sudden punctuations. Two such spectacular examples of dramatic reversals of growing worldwide interconnectivity include the fall of the Western Roman Empire in 476 CE (ushering the 'dark ages' in Europe) and the 20th-century interwar period (1918–39).

The prehistoric period (10,000 BCE–3500 BCE)

Let us begin roughly 12,000 years ago when small bands of hunters and gatherers reached the southern tip of South America.

This event marked the end of the long process of settling all five continents that was begun by our hominid African ancestors more than one million years ago. Although some major island groups in the Pacific and the Atlantic were not inhabited until relatively recent times, the truly global dispersion of our species was finally achieved. Completed by South American nomads, the success of this endeavour rested on the migratory achievements of their Siberian ancestors who had crossed the Bering Strait into North America at least 1,000 years earlier.

Even in this earliest phase of globalization, contact among thousands of hunter and gatherer bands occurred regularly while remaining geographically limited. This nomadic mode of social interaction changed dramatically about 10,000 years ago when humans took the crucial step of producing their own food. As a result of several factors, including the natural occurrence of plants and animals suitable for domestication as well as continental differences in area and total population size, only certain regions located on or near the vast Eurasian landmass proved to be ideal for these growing agricultural settlements. These areas were located in the Fertile Crescent, north-central China, North Africa, north-western India, and New Guinea. Over time, food surpluses achieved by these early farmers and herders led to population increases, the establishment of permanent villages, and the construction of fortified towns.

Over time, roving bands of nomads lost out to settled tribes, chiefdoms, and, ultimately, to powerful states based on agricultural food production (see Map 1). The decentralized, egalitarian nature of hunter and gatherer groups was replaced by centralized and highly stratified patriarchal social structures headed by chiefs and priests who were exempted from hard manual labour. Moreover, for the first time in human history, these farming societies were able to support two additional social classes whose members did not participate in food production. One group consisted of full-time craft specialists who directed

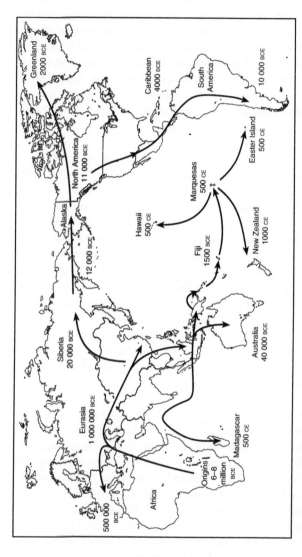

Map 1. Early human migration.

their creative energies toward the invention of new technologies, such as powerful iron tools, beautiful ornaments made of precious metals, complex irrigation canals, sophisticated pottery and basketry, and monumental building structures. The other group comprised professional priests, bureaucrats, and soldiers who played a key role in granting the monopolization of the means of violence to a few rulers; the precise accounting of food surpluses necessary for the growth and survival of the centralized state; the acquisition of new territory; the establishment of permanent trade routes; and the systematic exploration of distant regions.

For the most part, however, globalization in the prehistoric period was severely limited. Advanced forms of technology capable of overcoming existing geographical and social obstacles were largely absent. Thus, enduring long-distance interactions never materialized. It was only toward the end of this epoch that centrally administered forms of agriculture, religion, bureaucracy, and warfare slowly emerged as the key agents of intensifying modes of social exchange that would involve a growing number of societies in many regions of the world.

Perhaps the best way of characterizing the dynamic of this earliest phase of globalization would be to call it *the great divergence*—people and social connections stemming from a single origin but moving and diversifying greatly over time and across geographic space.

The premodern period (3500 BCE–1500 CE)

The invention of writing in Mesopotamia, Egypt, and central China between 3500 and 2000 BCE (see Figure 3) roughly coincided with the invention of the wheel around 3000 BCE in south-west Asia. Marking the close of the prehistoric period, these monumental inventions amounted to one of those technological and social boosts that shifted globalization into a higher gear. Thanks to the auspicious east–west orientation of Eurasia's major

23

3. Assyrian clay tablets with cuneiform writing, *c.*1900–1800 BCE.

continental axis—a geographic feature that had already facilitated the rapid spread of crops and animals suitable for food production along the same latitudes—the diffusion of these new technologies to distant parts of the continent occurred within only a few centuries. The importance of these inventions for the strengthening of globalization processes should be obvious. Among other things, the wheel spurred crucial infrastructural innovations such as animal-drawn carts and permanent roads that allowed for the faster and more efficient transportation of people and goods. In addition to the spread of ideas and inventions, writing greatly facilitated the coordination of complex social activities and thus encouraged large state formations. Of the sizeable territorial units that arose during this period, only the Andes civilizations of South America managed to grow into the mighty Inca Empire without the benefits of either the wheel or the written word.

The later premodern period was the age of empires. As some states succeeded in establishing permanent rule over others, the resulting vast territorial accumulations formed the basis of the Egyptian kingdoms, the Persian Empire, the Macedonian Empire, the American empires of the Aztecs and the Incas, the Roman

Empire, the Indian empires, the Byzantine Empire, the Islamic caliphates, the Holy Roman Empire, the African empires of Ghana, Mali, and Songhay, and the Ottoman Empire. All of these empires fostered the multiplication and extension of long-distance communication and the exchange of culture, technology, commodities, and diseases. The most enduring and technologically advanced of these vast premodern conglomerates was undoubtedly the Chinese Empire. A closer look at its history reveals some of the early dynamics of globalization.

After centuries of warfare among several independent states, the Qin Emperor's armies, in 221 BCE, finally unified large portions of north-east China. For the next 1,700 years, successive dynasties known as the Han, Sui, T'ang, Yuan, and Ming ruled an empire supported by vast bureaucracies that would extend its influence to such distant regions as tropical South-East Asia, the Mediterranean, India, and East Africa (see Figure 4). Dazzling artistry and brilliant philosophical achievements stimulated new discoveries in other fields of knowledge such as astronomy, mathematics,

4. The Great Wall of China.

and chemistry. The long list of major technological innovations achieved in China during the premodern period includes redesigned ploughshares, hydraulic engineering, gunpowder, the tapping of natural gas, the compass, mechanical clocks, paper, printing, lavishly embroidered silk fabrics, and sophisticated metalworking techniques. The construction of vast irrigation systems consisting of hundreds of small canals enhanced the region's agricultural productivity while at the same time providing for one of the best river transport systems in the world. The codification of law and the fixing of weights, measures, and values of coinage fostered the expansion of trade and markets. The standardization of the size of cart axles and the roads they travelled on allowed Chinese merchants for the first time to make precise calculations as to the desired quantities of imported and exported goods.

The most spectacular of these trade routes was the Silk Road. It linked the Chinese and the Roman empires, with Parthian traders serving as skilled intermediaries, and reached the Italian peninsula in 50 BCE. Even 1,300 years later, a truly multicultural group of Eurasian and African globetrotters—including the famous Moroccan merchant and scholar Ibn Battuta and his Venetian counterparts in the Marco Polo family—relied on this great Eurasian land route to reach the splendid imperial court of the Mongol khans in Beijing. As we noted in Chapter 1, China is currently working on the 21st-century renewal of the ancient Silk Road in the form of its massive One Belt One Road infrastructure project designed to connect Beijing to Western European cities.

By the 15th century CE, enormous Chinese fleets consisting of hundreds of 400-foot-long oceangoing ships were crossing the Indian Ocean and establishing short-lived trade outposts on the east coast of Africa. However, a few decades later, the rulers of the Chinese Empire implemented a series of fateful political decisions that halted overseas navigation and mandated a retreat from further technological development. This is another good example of the possible reversibility of globalization. The Chinese rulers cut short their empire's incipient industrial revolution, a development that allowed much smaller and less advanced European states to emerge as the primary historical agents behind the intensification of interconnectivity.

Toward the end of the premodern period, then, the existing global trade network (see Map 2) consisted of several interlocking trade circuits that connected the most populous regions of Eurasia and north-eastern Africa. Although both the Australian and the American continents still remained separate from this expanding web of economic, political, and cultural interdependence, the vast empires of the Aztecs and Incas had also succeeded in developing major trade networks in their own hemisphere.

The existence of these sprawling networks of economic and cultural exchange triggered massive waves of migration, which, in turn, led to further population increase and the rapid growth of urban centres. In the resulting cultural clashes, religions with only local significance were transformed into the major global religions we know today as Judaism, Christianity, Islam, Hinduism, and Buddhism. But higher population density and more intense social interaction over greater distances also facilitated the spread of new infectious diseases like the bubonic plague. An enormous epidemic of the mid-14th century, for example, killed up to one-third of the respective populations of China, the Middle East, and Europe. However, these unwelcome by-products of unfolding globalization processes did not reach their most horrific manifestation until the fateful 16th-century collision of the 'old' and 'new' worlds. Although the precise population size of the Americas before contact remains a contentious issue, it is estimated that the deadly germs of European invaders killed an estimated 18–20 million Native Americans—an inconceivable 90 to 95 per cent of the total indigenous population.

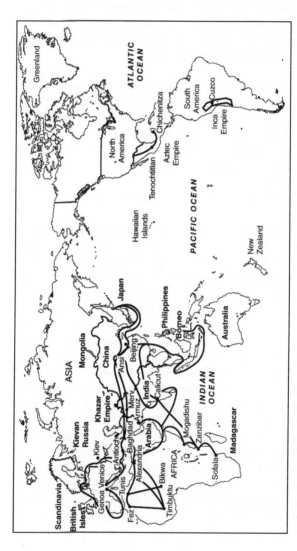

Map 2. Major world trade networks, 1000–1450.

The early modern period (1500–1750)

The term 'modernity' has become associated with the 18th-century European Enlightenment project of developing science, achieving a universal form of morality and law, and liberating rational modes of thought and social organization from the perceived irrationalities of myth, religion, and political tyranny. But it is important to acknowledge the existence of multiple forms of modernity that evolved in various parts of the world in resistance to European modernity. The label 'early modern', then, refers to the period between the European Renaissance and the height of the Enlightenment. During these two centuries, Europe and its social practices emerged as the primary catalyst for globalization after a long period of Asian predominance.

Indeed, having contributed little to technology and other civilizational achievements between about 500 CE and 1000 CE, Europeans north of the Alps greatly benefited from the diffusion of technological innovations originating in the Islamic and Chinese cultural spheres. Despite the weakened political influence of China and the noticeable ecological decline of the Fertile Crescent some 500 years later, European powers failed to penetrate into the interior of Africa and Asia. Instead, they turned their expansionistic desires westward, searching for a new, profitable sea route to India. Their efforts were aided by such innovations as mechanized printing, sophisticated wind and water mills, extensive postal systems, revised maritime technologies, and advanced navigation techniques. Add the enormous impact of the Reformation and the related liberal political idea of limited government and popular sovereignty, and we have identified the main forces behind the qualitative leap that greatly intensified demographic, cultural, ecological, and economic flows between Europe, Africa, and the Americas.

Of course, the rise of European metropolitan centres and their affiliated merchant classes represented another important factor responsible for strengthening globalization tendencies during the early modern period. Embodying the new values of individualism and unlimited material accumulation, European economic entrepreneurs laid the foundation of what later scholars would call the 'capitalist world system'. However, these fledgling merchant capitalists could not have achieved the global expansion of their commercial enterprises without substantial support from their respective governments. The monarchs of Spain, Portugal, the Netherlands, France, and England all put significant resources into the exploration of new worlds and the construction of new interregional markets that benefited them much more than their exotic 'trading partners'.

By the early 1600s, national joint stock companies like the Dutch and British East India companies were founded for the express purpose of setting up profitable overseas trade posts. As these innovative corporations grew in size and stature as a result of their exploitative practices, they acquired the power to regulate most intercontinental economic transactions, in the process implementing social institutions and cultural practices that enabled later colonial governments to place these foreign regions under direct political rule (see Figure 5). Related developments,

5. The sale of the island of Manhattan in 1626.

such as the Atlantic slave trade and forced population transfers within the Americas, resulted in the suffering and death of millions of non-Europeans while greatly benefiting white immigrants and their home countries.

To be sure, religious warfare within Europe also created its share of dislocation and displacement for Caucasian populations. Moreover, as a result of these protracted armed conflicts, military alliances and political arrangements underwent continuous modification. This highlights the crucial role of warfare as a catalyst of globalization. Evolving from the 1648 Westphalian peace treaty that ended the horrendous Thirty Years War that killed millions, the sovereign, territorial nation-state emerged in 18th-century Europe as the dominant framework of social life. As the early modern period drew to a close, contacts among nation-states were intensifying, creating both synergies and tensions.

The modern period (1750–1980s)

By the late 18th century, the great continent of Australia and the numerous Pacific islands were slowly incorporated into the European-dominated network of political, economic, and cultural exchange. Increasingly confronted with stories of 'distant lands' and images of exotic 'Others', Europeans and their migrant descendants on other continents took it upon themselves to assume the role of the world's guardians of civilization and morality. In spite of their persistent claims to universal leadership, however, the emerging middle classes perpetuated racist and sexist practices. Creating the foundation for what would become the capitalist economic system, they also tolerated appalling levels of inequality both within their own societies and between the global North and South. Fed by a steady stream of materials and resources that originated mostly in other regions of the world, Western capitalist countries underwent an unprecedented 'Industrial Revolution'. Daring to resist powerful governmental controls, economic entrepreneurs and their academic counterparts like Adam Smith began to spread a philosophy of individualism and rational self-interest that glorified the virtues of an idealized capitalist system supposedly based upon the providential workings of the free market and its *invisible hand*.

But the 19th century also saw the first forms of working-class resistance to the exploitative practices of industrial capitalism. Written in 1847 by the German political radicals Karl Marx and Friedrich Engels, a passage taken from their famous *Communist Manifesto* captures the enormous qualitative shift in social relations that kicked globalization into a higher gear (see Box 3).

Indeed, the volume of world trade increased dramatically between 1850 and 1914. Guided by the activities of multinational banks,

Box 3. Marx and Engels on globalization

The discovery of America prepared the way for mighty industry and its creation of a truly global market. The latter greatly expanded trade, navigation, and communication by land. These developments, in turn, caused the further expansion of industry. The growth of industry, trade, navigation, and railroads also went hand in hand with the rise of the bourgeoisie and capital which pushed to the background the old social classes of the Middle Ages... Chased around the globe by its burning desire for ever-expanding markets for its products, the bourgeoisie has no choice but settle everywhere; cultivate everywhere; establish connections everywhere... Rapidly improving the instruments of production, the bourgeoisie utilizes the incessantly easing modes of communication to pull all nations into civilization—even the most barbarian ones... In a nutshell, it creates the world in its own image. (Translated by the author) capital and goods flowed across the borders relatively freely as the sterling-based gold standard made possible the worldwide circulation of leading national currencies like the British pound and the Dutch guilder. Eager to acquire their own independent resource bases, most European nation-states subjected large portions of the global South to direct colonial rule. On the eve of the First World War during the so-called *belle époque* ('beautiful era'), merchandise trade measured as a percentage of gross national output totalled almost 12 per cent for the industrialized countries, a level unmatched until the 1970s. International pricing systems facilitated trade in important commodities like grains, cotton, and various metals. Brand name packaged goods like Coca-Cola drinks, Campbell soups, Singer sewing machines, and Remington typewriters made their first appearance. In order to raise the global visibility of these corporations, international advertising agencies launched the first full-blown trans-border commercial promotion campaigns.

As Marx and Engels noted, however, the rise of the European bourgeoisie and the related intensification of global interconnections would not have been possible without the 19th-century explosion of science and technology. To be sure, the maintenance of these new industrial regimes required new energy sources such as electricity and petroleum. The largely unregulated use of these power sources resulted in the annihilation of countless animal and plant species as well as the toxification of entire regions. On the upside, however, railways, mechanized shipping, and 20th-century intercontinental air transport turbocharged embodied and object-extended forms of mobility. Humanity was standing on the threshold of overcoming the last remaining geographical obstacles to the establishment of a genuine global infrastructure, while at the same time lowering transportation costs for goods and people alike.

These innovations in transportation were complemented by the swift development of communication technologies that served as the incubators of today's disembodied globalization. The telegraph and its transatlantic reach after 1866 provided for instant information exchanges between the two hemispheres. Moreover, the telegraph set the stage for the telephone and wireless radio communication, prompting newly emerging communication corporations like AT&T to coin advertising slogans in celebration of a world 'inextricably bound together'. Finally, the 20th-century arrival of mass circulation newspapers and magazines, film, and television further enhanced a growing consciousness of a rapidly shrinking world.

The modern period also witnessed an unprecedented population explosion. Having increased only modestly from about 300 million at the time of the birth of Christ to 760 million in 1750, the world's population reached 4.5 billion in 1980. Enormous waves of transcontinental migration intensified existing cultural exchanges and transformed traditional social patterns. Popular immigration countries like the United States of America, Canada, Australia, and New Zealand took advantage of this boost in human resources. By the early 20th century, America entered the world stage as a force to be reckoned with. At the same time, however, these migration countries experienced major cultural backlashes, causing their governments to make significant efforts to control these large migratory flows. In the process, they invented novel forms of bureaucratic control and developed new surveillance techniques designed to accumulate more information about 'nationals' while keeping 'aliens' out.

When the accelerating process of industrialization sharpened existing disparities in wealth and wellbeing beyond bearable limits in the early 20th century, many working people in the global North began to organize themselves politically in various labour movements and socialist parties. However, their idealistic calls for international class solidarity went largely unheeded. Instead, ideologies that translated the national imaginary into extremist political programmes captured the imagination of millions of people around the world. There is no question that interstate rivalries intensified in the 1930s as a result of the Great Depression, mass migration, urbanization, and industrial competition. This period of extreme nationalism culminated in the Second World War, genocides, and hostile measures to 'protect' narrowly conceived political communities that glorified cultural homogeneity.

The end of the Second World War saw the explosion of two powerful atomic bombs that killed more than 200,000 Japanese, most of them civilians. Nothing did more to convince people around the world of the impossibility of maintaining the illusion of geographically and politically separated 'nations'. A more positive result was the accelerating process of decolonization in the 1950s and 1960s that created new nation-states in the global South while at the same time intensifying global flows and international exchanges. A new political order of sovereign but interdependent nation-states anchored in the charter of the United Nations raised the prospect of global democratic governance. However, such internationalist hopes quickly faded as the Cold War divided the world for four long decades into two antagonistic spheres: a liberal-capitalist *First World* dominated by the United States, and an authoritarian-socialist *Second World* controlled by the Soviet Union. Both 'blocs' sought to establish their political and ideological dominance in what came to be known as the *Third World*.

Clearly this tripartite division of geography in terms of 'worlds' attests to the rise of a global imaginary. Thus, 'global' was not necessarily associated with positive meanings. After all, superpower confrontations like the 1962 Cuban Missile Crisis raised the spectre of a global conflict capable of destroying virtually all life on our planet. Indeed, this horrific moment of the world at the brink of annihilation found its permanent expression in the Cold War acronym MAD ('mutually assured destruction').

The contemporary period (from the 1980s)

As we noted at the beginning of this chapter, the dramatic creation, expansion, and acceleration of worldwide interdependencies and global consciousness that has occurred since the 1980s represents yet another quantum leap in the history of globalization. The best way of characterizing this latest globalization wave would be to call it *the great convergence*—different and widely spaced people and social connections coming together more rapidly than ever before. This dynamic received another boost with the 1991 collapse of the communist Soviet bloc and 'neoliberal' attempts to create an integrated global market. This deregulation of national economies, combined with the ICT Revolution, turbocharged globalization. As we discussed in Chapter 1, the unprecedented development of horizontal networks of digital communication connecting the local and global was made possible through the worldwide diffusion of the Internet, wireless communication, and digital social media.

But how, exactly, has globalization accelerated in these last three decades? What dimensions of social activity have been most affected by globalization? Is contemporary globalization a 'good' or a 'bad' thing? Is the explosion of populist movements around the world a sign that we are entering an age of 'deglobalization'? In the remaining chapters of this book, our exploration of the major dimensions of globalization will suggest possible answers to these crucial questions. In doing so, we will consciously limit the application of the term 'globalization' to the contemporary period while keeping in mind the main lesson of this chapter: the forces driving it can be traced back thousands of years.

Before we embark on the next stages of our globalization journey, let us pause and recall an important point we made in Chapter 1. Globalization is not a single process but a matrix of processes that operate simultaneously and unevenly in different forms—embodied, disembodied, object-extended, and organization-extended—across all geographical scales and across many dimensions. We could compare these interactions and interdependencies to the intricately connected parts of a powerful Ferrari V-12 engine. Yet, just as an apprentice car mechanic must turn off and disassemble this precious car engine in order to understand its operation, so must students of globalization switch off the complexity of the real-world flows and apply analytical distinctions in order to make sense of the massive assemblage of global interconnectivity.

Thus, in Chapters 3–8, we will examine the various domains of globalization in isolation; yet resist the temptation to reduce globalization to a single 'most important' aspect. Only in this way can we hope to avoid the blunder that kept the blind men from appreciating the elephant in its full glory.

Chapter 3
The economic dimension of globalization

In Chapters 1 and 2, we noted that evolving forms of digital technology configured around the Internet and social media are often considered the hallmarks of contemporary globalization. Indeed, technological progress of the magnitude seen in the last three decades is also a good indicator for the occurrence of profound social transformations centred on the *market*. Changes in the ways in which people undertake economic production and organize the exchange of commodities represent one obvious aspect of the great transformation of our age.

Economic globalization refers to the intensification and stretching of economic connections across the globe. Gigantic flows of capital mediated by digital technology and standardized means of transportation have stimulated trade in goods and services. Extending their reach around the world, markets have migrated to cyberspace and integrated local, national, and regional economies. Huge transnational corporations (TNCs), powerful international economic institutions, and gigantic regional business and trade networks like the Asian Pacific Economic Cooperation (APEC), the Association of Southeast Asian Nations (ASEAN), the Southern Common Market (MERCOSUR), and the European Union (EU) have emerged as the major building blocks of the 21st century's global economic order.

The emergence of the global economic order

Contemporary economic globalization can be traced back to the emergence of a new international economic order assembled at a watershed economic conference held towards the end of the Second World War in the sleepy New England town of Bretton Woods (see Figure 6). Under the leadership of the United States and Great Britain, the major powers of the global North agreed to reverse their protectionist policies of the interwar period. In addition to arriving at a firm commitment to expand trade, the participants of the conference also established binding rules on international economic activities. Moreover, they resolved to create a more stable monetary exchange system in which the value of each country's currency was pegged to a fixed gold value of the US dollar. Within these prescribed limits, however, individual nations were free to control the permeability of their borders.

6. The 1944 Bretton Woods Conference.

The Bretton Woods regime (BWR) also established three new international economic organizations. The International Monetary Fund (IMF) was created to administer the international monetary system. The International Bank for Reconstruction and Development, later known as the World Bank, was initially designed to provide loans for Europe's postwar reconstruction. During the 1950s, however, its purpose was expanded to fund various industrial projects in developing countries around the world. Finally, the General Agreement on Tariffs and Trade (GATT) was established in 1947 as a global trade organization charged with fashioning and enforcing multilateral trade agreements. In 1995, the World Trade Organization (WTO) was founded as the successor organization to GATT. By the turn of the century, the WTO had become the focal point of intense public controversy over the design and the effects of economic globalization.

In operation for almost three decades, the BWR contributed greatly to the establishment of what some observers have called the 'golden age of controlled capitalism' (1945–80). Trade and foreign direct investment (FDI) expanded faster than the world GDP and the share of exports in global output tripled from less than 5 per cent in 1945 to 16 per cent in 1981. Even conservative political parties in Europe and the United States embraced some version of state interventionism proposed by the celebrated British economist John Maynard Keynes, one of the chief architects of the BWR. A wage compromise between big business and labour together with strong mechanisms of state control over international capital movements made possible full employment and the expansion of the welfare state in the wealthy countries of the global North. Rising wages and increased social services secured a temporary class compromise that facilitated the expansion of the middle class.

In 1971, however, the BWR took a severe blow when President Richard Nixon abandoned the gold standard—the long-term basis for setting the rules of economic management based on stable rates of currency exchange—in response to profound political changes in the world that were undermining the economic competitiveness of US-based industries. The decade was characterized by global economic instability in the form of high inflation, low economic growth, high unemployment, public sector deficits, and two unprecedented energy crises due to the Organization of Petroleum Exporting Countries (OPEC)'s ability to control a large part of the world's oil supply. Progressive political forces in the global North most closely identified with the model of controlled capitalism suffered a series of spectacular election defeats at the hands of conservative political parties that advocated what came to be called a 'neoliberal' approach to economic and social policy (see Box 4).

In the 1980s, British Prime Minister Margaret Thatcher and US President Ronald Reagan emerged as the co-leaders of the

Box 4. Neoliberalism

Neoliberalism is rooted in the classical liberal ideals of Adam Smith (1723–90) and David Ricardo (1772–1823), British thinkers who viewed the market as a self-regulating mechanism tending toward equilibrium of supply and demand, thus securing the most efficient allocation of resources. These British philosophers considered that any constraint on free competition would interfere with the natural efficiency of market mechanisms, inevitably leading to social stagnation, political corruption, and the creation of unresponsive state bureaucracies. They also advocated the elimination of tariffs on imports and other barriers to trade and capital flows between nations. British sociologist Herbert Spencer (1820–1903) added to this doctrine a twist of social Darwinism by arguing that free market economies constitute the most civilized form of human competition in which the 'fittest' would naturally rise to the top.

neoliberal revolution against the Keynesian premise that the global economy works best when national governments are free to set their own political and economic agendas. Conversely, neoliberals asserted that releasing private economic activity from government control would provide a tremendous lift to world trade, investment, and living standards. To boost the legitimacy of their unorthodox ideas, pro-business elites in the global North consciously linked the novel term 'globalization' to a political agenda aimed at the 'liberation' and deregulation of state-regulated economies around the world. This budding neoliberal economic-political order received further legitimization with the 1989–91 collapse of communism in the Soviet bloc.

Since then, the three most significant dynamics related to accelerated economic globalization have been the internationalization of trade and finance, the increasing power of transnational corporations and large investment banks, and the role of international economic institutions like the IMF, the World Bank, and the WTO. In the remainder of this chapter, we will examine these important features of economic globalization as well as some of the challenges that have emerged in recent years.

The internationalization of trade and finance

Many people associate economic globalization with the controversial issue of free trade. After all, the total value of world trade exploded from $57 billion in 1947 to an astonishing $19.5 trillion in 2018. However, trade in goods and services has stagnated since the 2008 Global Financial Crisis (GFC). In fact, the 2018 KOF Globalization Index—a major index measuring primarily object-extended forms of globalization—recorded a downward movement in 2017, the first since 1975. The index is expected to flat-line or further decrease over the next several years. Often associated with globalization, increasing automation is estimated to result in anything from a 20 to a 30 per cent fall in global merchandise trade over the next decade. This raises the question whether we have reached *peak trade* and are approaching the limits of economic integration.

Ever since pro-trade tariff national populists came to power in the United States and some European countries in the 2010s, the public debate over the alleged benefits and drawbacks of free trade has been raging at a feverish pitch. Moreover, wealthy pro-market Northern governments and regional trading blocs have been hampered in their efforts to establish a single global market through far-reaching trade-liberalization agreements. For example, the protectionist Trump administration withdrew from the Trans-Pacific Partnership (TPP) in 2017. This far-reaching agreement would have established the largest free-trade trading bloc in the world. Still, the remaining eleven countries—including China, Canada, and Australia—managed to salvage the deal by signing a revised version of the treaty, called the Comprehensive and Progressive Agreement for Trans-Pacific Partnership.

While admitting that neoliberal sets of trade rules can override national legislation, a number of pro-free trade governments have held fast to the original neoliberal promise that the elimination or reduction of existing trade barriers among nations would increase global wealth and enhance consumer choice. The ultimate benefit of integrated markets, they argue, would be secure peaceful international relations and technological innovation for the benefit of all (see Box 5).

Indeed, there is evidence that some national economies have increased their productivity as a result of free trade. Millions of people have been lifted out of poverty in developing countries such as China, India, Vietnam, and Indonesia. As 2018 World Bank data show, the percentage of people living in extreme poverty (on less than $1.90 a day) fell from nearly 50 per cent in 1990 to an astonishing 8.6 per cent in 2016. Moreover, there are some clear material benefits that accrue to societies through

Box 5. Concrete neoliberal measures

1. Privatization of public enterprises.
2. Deregulation of the economy.
3. Liberalization of trade and industry.
4. Massive tax cuts.
5. 'Monetarist' measures to keep inflation in check, even at the risk of increasing unemployment.
6. Strict control on organized labour.
7. The reduction of public expenditures, particularly social spending.
8. The downsizing of government.
9. The expansion of international markets.
10. The removal of controls on global financial flows.

economic specialization, competition, and the massive spread of new technologies.

On the flipside, however, there are today still over 730 million people in the world living in extreme poverty. The UN recently announced that its target of bringing this number down to less than 250 million by 2030 will not be met. In addition, inequalities in income and wealth have skyrocketed especially *within* nations, suggesting that the benefits of neoliberal globalization accrue disproportionally at the top. As the 2018 Annual Oxfam Report shows, the 26 richest billionaires in the world own as many assets as the 3.8 billion people who make up the lower income half of the planet's population. While the number of billionaires has doubled in the decade since the 2008 GFC, the share of tax revenues paid by large corporations has dropped significantly. Finally, empirical data demonstrate that profits resulting from free trade have not been distributed fairly within and among various income groups. According to the US-based Economic Policy Institute, chief executives of America's top 350 companies earned 312 times

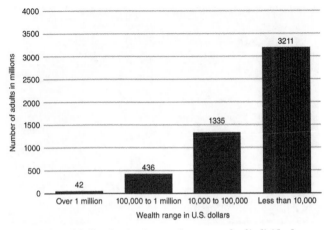

B. Global wealth distribution in 2018, by net worth of individuals (in millions).

more than the average worker in 2018. In 1965, the ratio of CEO to worker pay stood at only 20:1 (see Figure B).

The internationalization of trade has gone hand in hand with the liberalization of financial flows. Its key components include the deregulation of interest rates, the removal of credit controls, the privatization of government-owned banks and financial institutions, and the explosive growth of investment banking. Globalization of financial trading allows for increased mobility among different segments of the financial industry, with fewer restrictions and greater investment opportunities. Cutting-edge satellite systems and fibre-optic cables provided the nervous system of Internet-based technologies that further accelerated the liberalization of financial transactions. As captured by the snazzy title of Bill Gates's best-selling book at the turn of the 21st century, *business@the-speed-of-thought* has become commonplace today. Millions of individual investors utilize global real-time electronic investment networks not only to place their orders at the world's

7. The New York Stock Exchange.

leading stock exchanges, but also to receive valuable information about relevant developments (see Figure 7).

But a large part of the money involved in this *financialization of global capitalism* that swept the first decade of the new century had little to do with supplying capital for such productive investments as assembling machines or organizing raw materials and employees to produce saleable commodities. Most of the financial growth came from increases in lending in the property sector, often in the form of *high-risk hedge funds* and other purely money-dealing currency and securities markets, which seek profits from future production. In other words, investors were betting on commodities or currency rates that did not yet exist. Dominated by highly sensitive stock markets that drive high-risk innovation, the world's financial systems became characterized by high volatility, brutal competition, general insecurity, and even outright fraud. Global speculators often took advantage of weak financial and banking regulations to make astronomical profits in the emerging markets of developing countries. However, since these international capital flows can be reversed swiftly, they are capable of creating artificial boom-and-bust cycles that endanger the social welfare of entire regions. This is precisely what triggered the 1997–8 *Asian economic crisis* that caused havoc in the region.

A decade later, the increasing volatility of financial flows unleashed by three decades of neoliberal deregulation produced a global meltdown—the 2008 GFC—followed by an ongoing period of chronic economic instability. Similar to current trade-flow weaknesses, transnational bank flows and foreign-direct investment have stagnated at lower levels since the GFC. Cross-border financial flows have dipped from 22 per cent of world GDP in 2007 to merely 6 per cent in 2016—about the same level as in 1996. While the costs of communication have been falling quickly and consistently over the past decades, global transportation costs have proved to be more jittery and sluggish, plagued by uncertainty around highly volatile oil prices as well as unstable consumption patterns.

Before we continue our exploration of economic globalization with respect to the increasing power of TNCs and the enhanced role of international economic institutions, let us pause for a moment to examine briefly three crucial milestones in the evolution of the current era of global economic volatility: the 2008 GFC and the ensuing Great Recession; the European Sovereign Debt Crisis (ESDC) that came to a climax with the Greek government debt crisis during the 2010s; and the US–China trade conflict at the end of that decade.

A global era of economic volatility

The GFC has its roots in the 1980s and 1990s, when three successive US governments under Presidents Reagan, Bush I, and Clinton pushed for the significant deregulation of the domestic financial services industry. The neoliberal deregulation of US finance capital resulted in a frenzy of mergers that gave birth to huge financial-services conglomerates eager to plunge into securities ventures in areas that were not necessarily part of their underlying business. *Derivatives, financial futures, credit default swaps*, and other esoteric financial instruments became extremely popular when new computer-based mathematical models suggested more secure ways of managing the risk involved in buying an asset in the future at a price agreed to in the present. Relying far less on savings deposits, financial institutions borrowed from each other and sold these loans as securities, thus passing the risk on to investors in these securities. Other 'innovative' financial instruments such as hedge funds leveraged with borrowed funds fuelled a variety of speculative activities. Billions of investment dollars flowed into complex 'residential mortgage-backed securities' that promised investors up to a 25 per cent return on equity.

Assured by monetarist policies of the US Federal Reserve Bank aimed at keeping interest rates low and credit flowing abundantly, investment banks around the world eventually expanded their search for capital by buying risky *subprime loans* from mortgage brokers who, lured by the promise of big commissions, were accepting applications for housing mortgages with little or no down payment and without credit checks. Increasingly popular in the United States, most of these loans were adjustable-rate mortgages tied to fluctuations of short-term interest rates. Investment banks snapped up these high-risk loans knowing that they could resell these assets—and thus the risk involved—by bundling them into composite securities no longer subject to government regulation. Indeed, one of the most complex of these 'innovative' instruments of securitization—so-called *collateralized debt obligations*—often hid the problematic loans by bundling them together with lower-risk assets and reselling them to unsuspecting investors. Moreover, they were backed by positive credit ratings reports issued by credit ratings giants like Standard and Poor's and Moody's. The high yields flowing from these new securities funds attracted more and more investors around the world, thus rapidly globalizing more than US$1 trillion worth of what came to be known as 'toxic assets'.

In mid-2007, however, the financial steamroller finally ran out of fuel when seriously overvalued American real estate began to drop and foreclosures shot up dramatically. Some of the largest and most venerable financial institutions, insurance companies, and government-sponsored underwriters of mortgages such as Lehman Brothers, Bear Stearns, Merrill Lynch, Goldman Sachs, AIG, Citicorp, J. P. Morgan Chase, IndyMac Bank, Morgan Stanley, Fannie Mae, and Freddie Mac—to name but a few—either declared bankruptcy or had to be bailed out by the US taxpayers. Ultimately, both the conservative Bush II and the liberal Obama administrations found common ground in spending hundreds of billions of dollars on distressed mortgage securities, sometimes in return for a government share in the businesses involved.

Other industrialized countries followed suit with their own multi-billion dollar bailout packages, hoping that such massive injections of capital into ailing financial markets would help prop up financial institutions deemed 'too big to fail'. But one of the major consequences of the failing financial system was that banks trying to rebuild their capital base could hardly afford to keep lending large amounts of money (see Box 6). The flow of global credit froze to a trickle and businesses and individuals who relied on credit found it much more difficult to obtain. This credit shortage, in turn, impacted the profitability of many businesses, forcing them to cut back production and lay off workers. Industrial output declined, and unemployment shot up, as the world's stock markets dropped dramatically.

By 2009, the GFC had turned into what came to be known as the *Great Recession*: 14.3 trillion dollars, or 33 per cent of the value of the world's companies, had been wiped out. The developing world was especially hard hit by the declining demand for their exports. The leaders of the group of the world's twenty largest economies

(G20) met repeatedly in the early 2010s to devise a common strategy to forestall a global depression (see Map 3). Although most countries were slowly pulling out of the Great Recession, economic growth in many parts of the world remained anaemic and unemployment numbers came down only very slowly.

Soon it became clear that the GFC and its ensuing Great Recession had spawned a severe sovereign debt crisis and a banking crisis, especially in the EU. This rapidly escalating financial turmoil in the Eurozone not only threatened the fragile recovery of the global economy, but also came close to bankrupting the birthplace of Western civilization—Greece. What came to be known as the 'Greek debt crisis' began in 2009 and 2010 when the Greek government announced that it had understated its national budget deficits for years and was running out of funds. Shut out from borrowing in global financial markets, the IMF and ECB were forced to put together two gigantic bailout packages totalling $275 billion in order to avoid the country's financial collapse. But the EU lenders imposed harsh austerity terms in exchange for the loan, which caused further economic hardship and failed to restore economic stability. Greece's economy shrank by a quarter and the national unemployment rate shot up to 25 per cent. This disastrous economic development

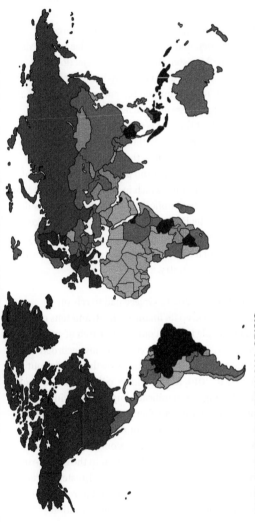

(2007–2009) WORLD FINANCIAL CRISIS

- Countries in official recession (two consecutive quarters)
- Countries in unofficial recession (one quarter)
- Countries with economic slowdown of more than 1.0%
- Countries with economic slowdown of more than 0.5%
- Countries with economic slowdown of more than 0.1%
- Countries with economic acceleration

(Between 2007 and 2008, as estimates of December 2008 by the International Monetary Fund)

Map 3. Countries falling into recession as a result of the Global Financial Crisis, 2007–2009.

exacerbated people's resentment of the neoliberal policies of austerity and sharpened the country's political polarization.

In 2015, Greece's left-leaning populist Syriza Party scored a surprising election victory, making its charismatic leader, Alexis Tsipras, the new Prime Minister. After multiple rejections of a tough bailout package proposed by Germany-led EU lenders and the defeat of a national referendum on the package by 61 per cent of the popular vote, Tsipras was nonetheless forced to bow to growing popular fears that the dire economic situation in the country would become even worse without the humiliating EU bailout package. After heated debates, the Greek parliament approved of the debt relief measure and promised to implement its highly contentious conditions, which included tax increases for farmers and major cuts in the public pension system. As a result of Greece's capitulation, the EU creditors offered an even larger multi-billion loan over three years, albeit with similar austerity conditions attached, which caused continuous political upheaval and unrest in the troubled country.

For the entire decade of the 2010s, Greece had to rely on international creditors to keep its finances afloat, and tens of thousands of young people left the country in search of greater economic opportunities. While the Greek economy recorded a modest turnaround reflected in an annual growth rate of about 2 per cent from 2017 to 2019, most ordinary citizens complained that they were not feeling any significant improvement in their lives. This enduring popular dissatisfaction corresponded to the country's stubbornly high unemployment rate of 18 per cent as late as 2019. As a result of these enduring economic woes, the Syriza Party lost the July 2019 national election to the centre-right Democracy Party in a landslide. The new Prime Minister, Kyriakos Mitsotakis, a Harvard-educated lawyer, promised to return the country to economic health as well as tighten immigration restrictions.

But Greece was only one among numerous nations that experienced major market declines in the current of global economic instability and volatility. The most surprising development occurred in early 2016 in the People's Republic of China—a country many observers consider the bastion of economic health accounting for over 9 per cent of world economic activity—when its stock markets went into free-fall. The Shanghai Composite and the Shenzhen Composite lost 5.3 per cent and 6.6 per cent, respectively, in less than a week. The turmoil in the Chinese markets caused equally sharp declines in stock exchanges around the world. After years of historic growth rates averaging 8 to 9 per cent, China's economy began to record less spectacular GDP increases around 6 to 7 per cent in ensuing years, yet its economic growth has remained ahead of that in Western countries.

This ominous 2016 slowdown in the Chinese economy coincided with the election of a protectionist American president. As the world's leading manufacturer, China was responsible for 12.8 per cent of global merchandise exports whereas the USA, the world's most voracious consumer, accounted for 13.2 per cent of global merchandise imports. In 2018, referring to this trade imbalance as the 'greatest theft in the history of the world—committed by China', President Donald Trump fired the opening shot in what threatened to become a full-blown trade war by announcing a 10 per cent tariff on $200 billion worth of Chinese goods. A year later, his administration slapped additional tariffs of up to 25 per cent on $250 billion worth of Chinese products and threatened to levy further tariffs worth $325 billion. It did not take long for China to impose retaliatory tariffs of up to 25 per cent on $110 billion worth of US goods, in the process, doubling duties on American agricultural and fish products from an average of 21 per cent to 42 per cent. In addition, President Xi Jinping threatened to implement punitive qualitative measures that would negatively affect US businesses operating in China.

Defiantly waging his trade battles outside the agreed-upon WTO framework, President Trump's tariff punishments were not reserved for China alone, but were also meted out to America's historically most reliable trading partners, Mexico, Canada, Japan, and the EU. At the time of this writing, the brewing trade war has already chilled global business investment. It has also raised fears of a global economic slowdown, thus signalling the continuation of a climate of global financial volatility that has existed since the 2008 GFC. Even the so-called 'economic boom' in the USA under the Trump administration that saw a significant rise of stock markets and a low unemployment rate of 3.6 per cent in mid-2019, is built upon mostly low-paying jobs in the service industry and other precarious and part-time jobs that have kept wages stagnant for nearly three decades. In the uncertain Brexit environment in the UK, matters were far worse. The country's annual rate of productivity growth averaged a dismal 0.4 per cent in the decade after the 2008 GFC, and inflation-adjusted wages have fallen sharply. In Chapter 8, we will return to a discussion of what these volatile economic dynamics might mean for the future of globalization.

The power of transnational corporations

Let us now return to our two remaining topics related to economic globalization: the growing power of TNCs and the enhanced role of international economic institutions. Contemporary versions of the early modern commercial enterprises we discussed in Chapter 2, TNCs are powerful enterprises comprising the parent company and subsidiary units in more than one country, which all operate under a coherent system of decision-making and a common strategy. Their numbers skyrocketed from 7,000 in 1970 to over 100,000 in 2018. Enterprises like Walmart, Sinopec Group, China National Petroleum, Royal Dutch Shell, Exxon-Mobil, and Toyota Motor belong to the 200 largest TNCs, which account for over half of the world's industrial output. None of these corporations maintains headquarters outside North America,

Mexico, Europe, China, Japan, and South Korea. This geographical concentration reflects existing asymmetrical power relations between the North and the South.

Rivalling nation-states in their economic power, these corporations control much of the world's investment capital, technology, and access to international markets (see Table 1). If we substituted 'revenue' for 'market value', five out of the top ten TNCs would be headquartered in China, including the No. 1 company: Industrial and Commercial Bank of China. Indeed, the gap between the USA and China is shrinking: the former has 575 companies listed on the 2019 Forbes Global 2000 list of the world's 2,000 largest TNCs compared to the latter's 309. Headquartered in 61 countries and accounting for combined revenues of more than US$40 trillion, these top-2,000 TNCs produced profits of $3.2 trillion, held assets worth $186 trillion, and represented a market value of $57 trillion.

In order to maintain their command posts in the global marketplace, TNCs frequently merge with their competitors. In 2018, TNCs spent over $4.6 trillion globally buying one another—the most since record-keeping began nearly four decades ago. Some of these recent mega-mergers include the US$130 billion marriage of Dow Chemical and DuPont in 2015; the 'mother of all beer mergers' uniting Anheuser-Busch InBev with SABMiller for the proud amount of US$105 billion in 2015; the US$278 billion consolidation of China's biggest coal miner, Shenhua Group, with China Guodian Corporation, the country's largest coal-fired power generators, in 2017; and the US$121 billion union of United Technologies (Aerospace Division) with giant arms manufacturer and major US defence contractor Raytheon in 2019.

TNCs have consolidated their global operations in what has remained a largely deregulated global labour market. The availability of cheap labour, resources, and favourable production

Table 1. Transnational corporations versus countries: a comparison (2018)

Corporation	Industry/Headquarters	Market value (in US$ billion)	Country (global GDP rank)	GDP (in US$ billion)
1. Apple	Computer hardware	725	Turkey (18)	722
2. Exxon Mobil	Oil and gas operations	357	Austria (30)	373
3. Berkshire Hathaway	Investment services, USA	356	United Arab Emirates (31)	339
4. Google	Computing services, USA	346	South Africa (32)	317
5. Microsoft	Computing software & programming, USA	334	Malaysia (33)	313
6. PetroChina	Oil & gas operations	330	Hong Kong (34)	308
7. Wells Fargo	Banking & finance, USA	280	Colombia (39)	274
8. Johnson & Johnson	Medical equipment & supplies, USA	279.7	Pakistan (40)	271
9. Industrial & Commercial Bank of China	Banking & finance, China	275	Chile (41)	240
10. Novartis	Pharmaceuticals, Switzerland	268	Finland (42)	231

Sources: created using data taken from Statista, 2019: <https://www.statista.com/statistics/263264/top- companies-in-the-world-by-market-value/>; Knoema World GDP Rankings 2018: <https://knoema.com/nwnfkne/world-gdp-ranking-2018-gdp-by-country-data-and-charts>; Forbes Global 2000: <http://www.forbes.com/global2000/#1150f879335d>

conditions in the global South has enhanced corporate mobility and profitability. Accounting for over 70 per cent of world trade, TNCs are responsible for massive foreign direct investments (FDI). As the 2019 UNCTAD *World Investment Report* shows, global FDI undertaken by transnational enterprises in 2019 is expected to amount to $1.5 trillion.

No doubt, the immense power of TNCs has profoundly altered the structure and functioning of the world economy. These giant firms and their global strategies have become major determinants of trade flows, the location of industries, and other economic activities around the world. In particular, their ability to disperse manufacturing processes into many discrete phases carried out in many different locations around the world has globalized economic production. Immense transnational production networks allow TNCs like Walmart, General Motors, or Volkswagen to break down the production process into detachable component phases that can be dispersed throughout the world. Such 'global value chains' also allow for a faster and more efficient distribution and marketing of their products on a global scale (see Map 4).

A groundbreaking study published in 2011 analysed the relationships between 43,060 large TNCs in terms of share ownerships linking them. The findings revealed that a relatively small core of 1,318 corporations appeared to own collectively through their shares the majority of the world's large blue chip and manufacturing firms. In fact, an even smaller number of these TNCS—147 super-connected corporations, to be exact—controlled 40 per cent of the total wealth in the network. Most of them were financial institutions like Barclays Bank, which topped the list. Ironically, it was this very bank that found itself at the centre of a huge scandal that rocked the financial world in July 2012, when it was revealed that Barclays and fifteen other major banks had rigged the world's most important global interest rate for years. Similarly, Walmart admitted in 2019 to violating the US Foreign Corrupt Practices Act by making illegal bribery payments to

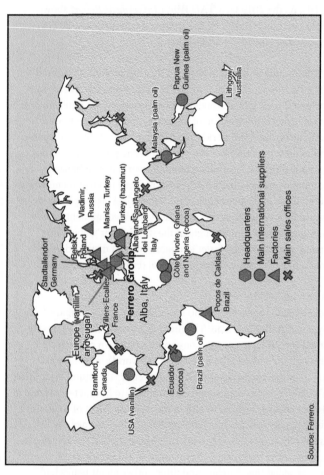

Map 4. The Nutella® Global Value Chain.

Source: Ferrero.

58

foreign government officials in order to open new production locations around the globe at extremely favourable terms. Walmart's guilty plea resulted in a US$282 million fine, a rather paltry figure compared to its massive US$7 billion profit generated in 2018.

The enhanced role of international economic institutions

The three international economic institutions most frequently mentioned in the context of economic globalization are the IMF, the World Bank, and the WTO. These institutions enjoy the privileged position of making and enforcing the rules of a global economy that is sustained by significant power differentials between the global North and South. Since we will discuss the WTO in some detail in Chapter 7, let us focus here on the other two institutions. As pointed out, the IMF and the World Bank emerged from the BWR. During the Cold War, their important function of providing loans for developing countries became connected to the West's political objective of containing communism. Starting in the 1970s, and especially after the fall of the Soviet Union, the economic agenda of the IMF and the World Bank largely supported neoliberal interests to integrate and deregulate markets around the world (see Box 7).

In return for supplying much-needed loans to developing countries, the IMF and the World Bank demand from their creditor nations the implementation of so-called *structural adjustment programmes* (SAPs). Unleashed on developing countries in the 1990s, this set of neoliberal policies is often referred to as the 'Washington Consensus' (WC). It was devised and codified by John Williamson, who was an IMF adviser in the 1970s. The various sections of the WC were mainly directed at countries with large foreign debts remaining from the 1970s and 1980s. The official purpose of Williamson's framework was to reform the internal economic mechanisms of debtor countries in

Box 7. Nokia's role in the Finnish economy

Named after a small town in south-west Finland, Nokia Corporation rose from modest beginnings in 1871 to become the world's largest TNC engaged in the manufacturing of mobile phones and converging Internet industries. In 1998, Nokia sold a record 41 million cellular phones worldwide. At the turn of the century, its products connected more than a billion people in an invisible web around the globe. The engine of Finland's economy, Nokia employed 22,000 Finns—not counting the 20,000 domestic employees who worked for companies that depended on Nokia contracts. The corporation represented two-thirds of the stock market's value and one-fifth of the nation's total export. However, Nokia's gift to Finland—the distinction of being the most interconnected nation in the world—came at the price of economic dependency. The corporation produced a large part of Finland's tax revenue, and its annual sales almost equalled the entire national budget.

Yet, when Nokia's growth rate slowed in the late 2000s in the wake of the GFC—10,000 employees were let go in 2012 and some Finnish factories shut down—company executives successfully pressured the Finnish government to reduce its corporate tax rates. Many Finnish citizens complained that such influence wielded by relatively few Nokia managers translated into tax concessions that adversely affected the country's generous and egalitarian welfare system. After further economic setbacks that translated into more layoffs, Nokia sold its mobile phone business to Microsoft in 2014. However, the tax concessions it had received from the Finnish government bought the company the time it needed to design and implement a new business plan focused on network equipment and innovative wireless technology. The success of this strategy was reflected in Nokia's subsequent US$20 billion acquisition of the French telecommunications company Alcatel-Lucent and its return to the mobile and smartphone market in 2017. By 2018, its workforce had rebounded to over 103,000 employees across 130 countries and the company reported revenue of US$26 billion.

the developing world so that they would be in a better position to repay the debts they had incurred. In practice, however, the terms of the WC spelled out a new form of colonialism. Its ten points, as defined by Williamson, required governments to implement the following SAPs in order to qualify for loans:

1   A guarantee of fiscal discipline, and a curb to budget deficits.
2   A reduction of public expenditure, particularly in the military and public administration.
3   Tax reform, aiming at the creation of a system with a broad base and with effective enforcement.
4   Financial liberalization, with interest rates determined by the market.
5   Competitive exchange rates, to assist export-led growth.
6   Trade liberalization, coupled with the abolition of import licensing and a reduction of tariffs.
7   Promotion of foreign direct investment.
8   Privatization of state enterprises, leading to efficient management and improved performance.
9   Deregulation of the economy.
10   Protection of property rights.

It is no coincidence that this programme is called the WC, for, from the outset, the United States has been the dominant power in the IMF and the World Bank.

Unfortunately, however, large portions of the 'development loans' granted by these institutions have either been pocketed by authoritarian political leaders in the global South or have enriched local businesses and the Northern corporations they usually serve. Sometimes, exorbitant sums are spent on ill-considered construction projects. Most importantly, however, SAPs rarely produce the desired result of developing debtor societies, because mandated cuts in public spending translate into fewer social programmes, reduced educational opportunities, more environmental pollution, and greater poverty for the vast majority of people.

Typically, the largest share of the developing countries' national budget is spent on servicing their outstanding debts. In fact, the total external debt of emerging and developing countries skyrocketed from US$70.2 billion in 1970 to US$6.8 trillion in 2013. A 2018 analysis from Jubilee Debt Campaign shows that average government external debt payments across the 126 developing countries for which data were available have increased to 10.7 per cent of government revenue in 2017, the highest level since 2004. According to comprehensive World Bank and OECD data, developing countries paid out, in 2010, $184 billion in debt service while receiving only $134 billion in aid. That year, the public external debt of the global South had reached $1.6 trillion. This sounds like a lot of money, but it represents only 5 per cent of the estimated $29 trillion the US government spent on the bailout of the banks in the wake of the 2008 GFC. Pressured for decades by anti-corporate globalist forces like the Committee for the Abolition of Third-World Debt or the Jubilee Debt Campaign, the IMF and the World Bank have only recently been willing to consider a new policy of blanket debt forgiveness in special cases.

As this chapter has shown, economic perspectives on globalization can hardly be discussed apart from an analysis of political processes and institutions. After all, the intensification of global economic interconnections—as well as recent challenges to it—does not simply fall from the sky. Rather, it is a set of processes put into motion together with a series of related political decisions. Hence, while acknowledging the importance of economics in our exploration of globalization, this chapter nonetheless ends with the suggestion that we ought to be sceptical of one-sided accounts that identify expanding economic activity as the primary aspect of globalization. For example, the impact of *politics* on the forging of global interconnectivity demands that we flesh out in more detail the political dimension of globalization.

Chapter 4
The political dimension of globalization

Political globalization refers to the intensification and expansion of political interrelations across the globe. These processes raise an important set of political issues pertaining to the principle of state sovereignty, the growing impact of intergovernmental organizations, the future prospects for regional and global governance, and global migration flows. Obviously, these themes respond to the evolution of political arrangements beyond the framework of the nation-state, thus breaking new conceptual and institutional ground.

For the last two centuries, humans have organized their political differences along territorial lines that generated a sense of 'belonging' to a particular nation-state. Based on 17th-century European principles of sovereignty and territoriality, the modern nation-state system found its mature expression at the end of the First World War in US President Woodrow Wilson's famous *Fourteen Points* of national self-determination. But Wilson's assumption that all forms of national identity should be given their territorial expression in a sovereign nation-state proved to be extremely difficult to enforce in practice. Moreover, by enshrining the nation-state as the ethical and legal pinnacle of his proposed interstate system, he unwittingly lent some legitimacy to those radical ethnonationalist forces that pushed the world into the Second World War.

This artificial division of planetary social space into 'domestic' and 'foreign' spheres corresponds to people's national imaginary that engenders collective identities based on the creation of a common 'us' versus an unfamiliar 'them'. Thus, the modern nation-state system has rested on psychological foundations and cultural assumptions that convey a sense of existential security and historic continuity of the national, while at the same time demanding from its citizens that they put their patriotic loyalties to the ultimate test. Nurtured by demonizing images of 'outsiders' and 'foreigners', people's belief in the superiority of their own nation has supplied the psychological energy required for large-scale warfare—just as the enormous productive capacities of the modern state have provided the material means necessary to fight the costly *total wars* of the last century.

President Wilson's other main idea of a *League of Nations* that would give international cooperation an institutional expression was belatedly realized with the founding of the *United Nations* in 1945 (see Figure 8). While deeply rooted in a political order based on the modern nation-state system, the UN and other fledgling intergovernmental organizations also served as catalysts for the gradual extension of political activities across national boundaries, thus simultaneously affirming and undermining the principle of national sovereignty.

As globalization tendencies grew stronger during the 1970s and 1980s, the international order of separate nation-states encountered a worldwide web of political interdependencies that challenged conventional forms of national sovereignty. Noticing these tendencies, many globalization experts have suggested that the period since the 1990s has been marked by a radical deterritorialization of politics, rule-making, and governance. In fact, early *hyperglobalist* best-sellers on the subject—for example, Japanese management consultant Kenichi Ohmae's *The End of the Nation State* (1995) or *New York Times* columnist Thomas Friedman's *The Lexus and the Olive Tree* (1999)—left their readers

8. The Security Council of the United Nations in session.

with the image of globalization as an irreversible juggernaut
flattening the nation-state. Considering such pronouncements
premature at best and erroneous at worst, *globalization sceptics*
have not only affirmed the continued dominance of the nation-state
as the political container of modern social life but also pointed to
the emergence of regional blocs as evidence for new forms of
subglobal territorialization. Some of these critics have gone so far
as to suggest that globalization is actually accentuating people's
attachment to the principle of nationality. Each of these two
perspectives—hyperglobalist and sceptical—offers different
assessments of the fate of the modern nation-state based on
diverging views on the relative importance of political factors.

Out of these disagreements there have emerged three fundamental
questions that probe the extent of political globalization. First, is it
really true that the power of the nation-state has been curtailed by
massive flows of capital, people, and technology across territorial
boundaries? Second, are the primary causes of these flows to be
found in politics or in economics? Third, are we witnessing the

emergence of new global governance structures? This chapter will consider them in turn.

The demise of the nation-state?

Hyperglobalizers like Ohmae and Friedman respond to this question affirmatively. After all, they consider political globalization a mere secondary phenomenon driven by more fundamental economic and technological forces. Hyperglobalizers argue that politics has been rendered almost powerless by an unstoppable techno-economic juggernaut that will crush all governmental attempts to reintroduce restrictive policies and regulations. Endowing economics with an inner logic apart from, and superior to, politics, these commentators look forward to a new phase in world history in which the main role of government will be to serve as a superconductor for global capitalism.

Pronouncing the rise of a 'borderless world', hyperglobalizers seek to convince the public that globalization inevitably involves the decline of bounded territory as a meaningful concept for understanding political and social change. Consequently, they suggest that political power is located in global social formations and expressed through global networks rather than through territorially based states. In fact, they argue that nation-states have already lost their dominant role in the global economy. As territorial divisions are becoming increasingly irrelevant, states are even less capable of determining the direction of social life within their borders. For example, since the workings of genuinely global capital markets dwarf their ability to control exchange rates or protect their currency, nation-states have become vulnerable to the discipline imposed by economic choices made on a supranational level.

Globalization sceptics like Paul Hirst and Grahame Thompson disagree, highlighting instead the central role of politics in unleashing the forces of globalization, especially through the successful mobilization of political power. In their view, the rapid expansion of global economic activity can be reduced neither to a natural law of the market nor to the development of computer technology. Rather, it originates with political decisions made by neoliberal national governments from the late 1970s to the 1990s to lift international restrictions on capital. Once those decisions were implemented, worldwide markets and new technologies came into their own. The clear implication of this perspective is that national territory still matters. Hence, sceptics insist on the continued relevance of conventional political units that operate in the form of either modern nation-states or world cities linked to national units.

The arguments of both hyperglobalizers and sceptics remain entangled in a particularly vexing version of the chicken-and-the-egg problem. After all, economic forms of interdependence are set in motion by political decisions, but these decisions are nonetheless made in particular economic contexts. As we noted, the economic and political aspects of globalization are profoundly interconnected. For example, it has become much easier for capital to escape taxation schemes and other national policy restrictions. In 2016, the *Panama Papers*—a leaked set of nearly 12 million confidential documents—revealed how wealthy individuals, including government officials, managed to evade national income taxes by hiding their assets in Panamanian offshore companies. Moreover, global markets frequently undermine the capacity of governments to set independent national policy objectives and impose their own domestic standards. While it seems obvious to acknowledge the decline of the nation-state as a sovereign entity and the ensuing devolution of state power to both local governments and supranational institutions, the current surge of national populist political forces discussed in Chapter 7 suggests that political globalization is not an irreversible process.

Political globalization and migration

Again, the relative decline of the nation-state over the last three decades does not necessarily mean that governments have become impotent bystanders to the workings of global forces. States can still take significant measures to make their economies more or less attractive to global investors. In addition, they have continued to retain control over education, infrastructure, and foreign policy. Still, the intensifying population movements linked to the form of embodied globalization have challenged some of the most crucial powers of nation-states: immigration control, population registration, and security protocols. The number of international migrants reached 258 million in 2017, with an increase of 85 million since 2000 (see Figure C). With about 3.4 per cent of the world's population living outside their country of origin, immigration control has become a central issue in most advanced nations. Many governments seek to restrict population flows, particularly those originating in the poor countries of the global South. Even in the United States, significant annual inflows of about 1.2 million legal permanent immigrants during the 2010s are less than the levels recorded during the first two decades of the 20th century.

In order to illustrate the growing problems of nation-states to cope with increasing trans-border migration flows, let us consider a recent example: the *Syrian refugee crisis*. It started in the early 2010s when the Syrian dictator Bashar al-Assad, backed by Russian President Vladimir Putin, embarked on a confrontational course with pro-democracy 'Arab Spring' demonstrators whom he vilified as 'rebel forces'. The country quickly descended into an all-out civil war that would kill more than 250,000 people over the next five years. The relentless fighting triggered a humanitarian crisis of truly epic proportions. By 2016, nearly 6 million Syrians—out of a total population of 23 million—had been internally displaced. Close to 5 million people had fled

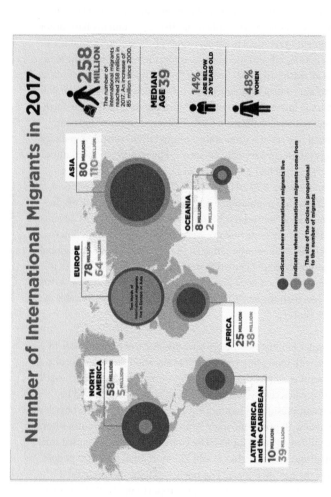

C. Number of international migrants, 2017. (Unknown residuals were redistributed proportionally to the size of groups for which data on international migrants were available by origin.)

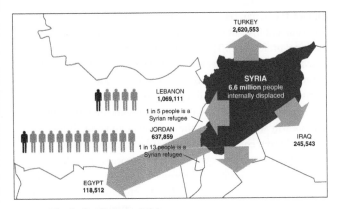

Map 5. The Syrian Refugee Crisis.

the country in search of both personal safety and economic opportunity (see Map 5). The majority of Syrian refugees ended up in camps in the neighbouring countries of Jordan, Lebanon, Iraq, and Turkey. But more than a million people attempted the dangerous trip across the Mediterranean from Turkey to Greece, hoping to find a better future in the prosperous states of the European Union.

Germany, in particular, emerged as their preferred place of refuge. The conservative German government under Chancellor Angela Merkel showed tremendous courage and compassion by welcoming over 1 million political refugees in 2015 alone—half of whom hailed from Syria. In order to reach their destination, Syrian migrants had to embark on a long route that led them from Greece across Macedonia, Serbia or Croatia, Hungary or Slovenia, and Austria, until they finally arrived in Bavaria, hoping for a swift approval of their residence applications. Even though some EU countries like Hungary resorted to rather inhumane policies and drastic measures to keep refugees out of their territory, their hastily erected border fences stretching over many miles ultimately proved to be ineffective in stopping such gigantic population movements.

In fact, the Syrian refugee crisis revealed the inadequacy of the EU's current institutional immigration arrangements based on national preferences. The so-called *Schengen Agreement* that provided for open borders among EU core countries lacked the robustness and comprehensiveness necessary for coping with this crisis situation. As policy differences among various national governments became more pronounced, some member countries temporarily withdrew from the agreement and reinstituted stricter border controls. Others placed arbitrary limits on the number of refugees they were willing to process and refused to consider a more coordinated approach. Unable to deal with the huge influx of migrants, the EU faced a predicament that laid bare deep political divisions over regional migration policy among member states.

Moreover, the Syrian refugee crisis also made visible existing cultural fissures and religious biases. For example, a number of official government ministers in EU member states like Poland, Slovakia, and Hungary openly expressed their opposition to the 'Islamization of Europe' and stated their preference for a small number of Christian refugees. Countries like Germany and Austria, on the other hand, experienced a polarization of public sentiments with roughly even numbers of citizens supporting or opposing more liberal political asylum measures. There is also much evidence that the pro-Brexit forces in the UK used the Syrian refugee crisis in their 2016 referendum campaign to convince the British people that the only way to stop mass immigration was to leave the EU.

But the Syrian refugee crisis represents only one case among many similar migration dynamics. According to the latest UN figures, a record 71 million refugees were displaced worldwide in 2018. Examples include the forced expulsion of an estimated 700,000 Rohingya people—an Islamic minority in Myanmar excluded from citizenship—as well as hundreds of thousands of Central American refugees who have sought political asylum in the USA.

The latter case, in particular, has drawn much attention because it involves one of the world's most liberal immigration countries applying a so-called *zero-tolerance approach* designed to deter illegal migration by legitimate political refugees seeking to escape the deadly violence in their home countries. In fact, the Trump administration has gone so far as to separate thousands of children from their families. Kept under egregious conditions in migrant detention facilities that have been compared to 'concentration camps' by some critics, many of these children were even transferred into foster care placement across the USA—without their parents' permission and no adequate tracking mechanisms that would allow for a safe reunion with their families (see Figure 9).

Finally, the intensifying global migration dynamics also play into crucial issues of *national security*. For example, the heinous attacks of global terrorist networks affiliated with jihadist Islamist groups like ISIL or al-Shabaab—such as the 2017 Manchester

9. **Central American migrants, including children, behind the fence of a makeshift US detention centre in El Paso, Texas, 29 March 2019.**

Arena bombing, the 2018 suicide bombings in the Nigerian city of Mubi, or the deadly 2019 Sri Lanka Easter bombings—have revealed the inadequacy of conventional national security routines and protocols. As a result, the globalization of terrorist and crime networks has forced national governments to engage in new forms of international cooperation. Thus, we can observe the seemingly paradoxical effect of political globalization: while states still matter, they are increasingly forced into new transnational practices that undermine their old claims to sovereignty and non-interference (see Box 8).

In summary, then, we ought to reject premature pronouncements of the impending demise of the nation-state, while also acknowledging its increasing difficulties in performing many of its traditional functions. Contemporary globalization has weakened some of the conventional boundaries between domestic and foreign policies while fostering the growth of supraterritorial social spaces and institutions that, in turn, unsettle both familiar political arrangements and cultural traditions. As the 21st century wears on, people around the world will become more conscious of the fact that they live in a transitional era in which the modern nation-state system will be increasingly challenged by global problems that require strengthening the dynamics of global governance structures.

Political globalization and global governance

Political globalization is perhaps most visible in the rise of supraterritorial institutions and associations like the International Criminal Court or the International Law Commission held together by common norms and interests (see Figure D). In this early phase of *global governance*, these structures resemble an eclectic network of interrelated power centres such as municipal and provincial authorities, regional blocs, international organizations, and national and international private-sector associations.

Box 8. Losing national control? Russia's interference in the 2016 US Presidential election

The Russian government's systematic and sweeping attempts to influence the 2016 US presidential election in favour of Donald Trump represents another instructive case of how nation-states are struggling to maintain control over even their most basic functions such as the organization and management of open and fair national elections. Consider the following short excerpt from the official 2019 report issued by Special Counsel Robert S. Mueller III:

Evidence of Russian government operations began to surface in mid-2016. In June, the Democratic National Committee and its cyber response team publicly announced that Russian hackers had compromised its computer network. Releases of hacked materials that public reporting soon attributed to the Russian government began that same month. Additional releases followed in July through the organization WikiLeaks, with further releases in October and November...As set forth in detail in this report, the Special Counsel's investigation established that Russia interfered in the 2016 presidential election principally through two operations. First, a Russian entity carried out a social media campaign that favored presidential candidate Donald J. Trump and disparaged presidential candidate Hillary Clinton. Second, a Russian intelligence service conducted computer-intrusion operations against entities, employees, and volunteers working on the Clinton Campaign and then released stolen documents.

On the municipal and provincial level, there has been a remarkable growth in the number of policy initiatives and transborder links between various substate authorities. For example, Chinese provinces and US federal states have established permanent missions and points of contact, some of which operate relatively autonomously with little oversight from their respective

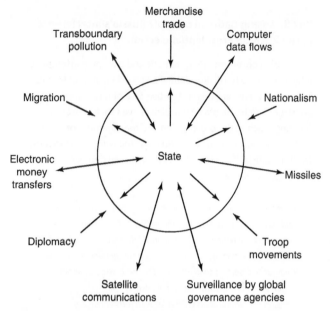

D. The nation-state in a globalizing world.

national governments. Various provinces and federal states in
Canada, India, and Brazil are developing their own trade
agendas and financial strategies to obtain loans. An example of
international cooperation on the municipal level is the rise of
powerful city networks such as the World Association of Major
Metropolises that develop cooperative ventures to deal with
common local issues across national borders. So-called *global
cities*—Hong Kong, London, New York, Shanghai, Singapore,
Sydney, Tokyo, and many others—are in some respects more
closely connected to each other than they are to their national
governments.

On the regional level, there has been an extraordinary proliferation
of multilateral organizations and agreements. Regional clubs and
transnational agencies such as APEC or ASEAN have sprung up

across the world, leading some observers to speculate that regional networks will eventually replace nation-states as the basic unit of governance. Starting out as attempts to integrate regional economies, these blocs have, in some cases, already evolved into loose political federations with common institutions of governance. For example, the European common market began in 1950 with French Foreign Minister Robert Schuman's modest plan to create a supranational institution charged with regulating French and German coal and steel production. Seven decades on, the twenty-eight member states of the EU form a close community with some shared political institutions that create common public policies and design binding security arrangements. In the first decade of the 21st century, several formerly communist countries joined the EU, which now extends as far to the east as Latvia, Romania, and Cyprus (see Map 6). But, as we discuss further in Chapter 8, such an expansionist dynamic is by no means inexorable. The 2016 UK referendum in favour of Brexit—and the ensuing bitter and drawn-out political battle over the conditions of its implementation—is a clear illustration that even a decade-long process of regionalization can be halted and possibly reversed.

On a global level, governments have formed a number of international organizations, including the UN, NATO, WTO, and OECD. Full legal membership in these organizations is open to states only, and the decision-making authority lies with representatives from national governments. The proliferation of these transnational bodies has shown that nation-states find it increasingly difficult to manage sprawling networks of social interdependence.

Finally, the emerging structure of global governance has been shaped by *global civil society*—a shared social realm populated by thousands of voluntary, non-governmental associations of worldwide reach. International NGOs such as Doctors Without Borders or Greenpeace represent millions of ordinary citizens who

Map 6. The European Union, 2019.

are prepared to challenge political and economic decisions made by nation-states and intergovernmental organizations.

One concrete example of the growing significance of INGOs in managing increasing global interconnectivity was the role of *Médecins Sans Frontières*/Doctors Without Borders (MSF/DWB) during the dramatic outbreak of the Ebola virus disease in West Africa from December 2013 to early 2016. Made up mainly of doctors and health sector workers from around the world who volunteer their services at any location on earth, MSF/DWB provides assistance to populations in distress such as victims of natural and man-made disasters, and armed conflict. It observes neutrality and impartiality in the name of its universal medical code of ethics and also maintains complete independence from all political, economic, and religious powers.

When Ebola—one of the world's most deadly diseases that can kill up to 90 per cent of those stricken—hit in the West African countries of Guinea, Sierra Leone, and Liberia in late 2013, MSF/DWB was among the first responders on the ground, much earlier than many of the aid initiatives organized by the UN or individual nation-states. At its peak, MSF/DWF employed nearly 4,000 national staff and 325 expat staff in West Africa to combat a disease that threatened to turn into a global pandemic, especially when isolated cases of virus transmission were reported in North America and Europe. By the time the WHO declared an official end to the Ebola epidemic in January 2016, MSF/DWB had treated more than 10,000 patients in dozens of their management centres in the region. Given the lack of political will by national and local governments to rapidly deploy assistance to help affected communities in West Africa, the activities of NGOs like MSF/DWB proved to be decisive in preventing what could have easily turned into an unprecedented catastrophe of global proportions.

The Ebola crisis in West Africa demonstrated that more coordinated international steps have to be taken to better prepare the world for a future disease outbreak. Unfortunately, these measures were not implemented as a result of a major shortfall in the WHO's global contingency fund. Promptly, the Ebola virus struck Africa again in 2019—this time in the Democratic Republic of Congo, a country plagued by persistent violent conflicts and neglected for decades by the international community. More than 1,500 people died in the first half of 2019, and thousands more have been infected (see Figure 10). As the outbreak is poised to spread into neighbouring Uganda and possibly South Sudan, an unstable country dotted with refugee camps, it threatens to escape containment and turn into a major calamity for the region. Once again, it appears

10. Health workers in the Democratic Republic of Congo burying a victim of the Ebola virus, June 2019.

that INGOs like MSF/DWB will have to play a major role in preventing the worst.

As a result of the tough lessons learned in the struggle against pandemics and other global problems, some Global Studies experts believe that political globalization might facilitate the strengthening of democratic transnational social forces anchored in this thriving sphere of global civil society. Predicting that democratic rights will ultimately become detached from their narrow relationship to discrete territorial units, these optimistic voices anticipate the creation of a democratic global governance structure based on Western cosmopolitan ideals, international legal arrangements, and a web of expanding linkages between various governmental and non-governmental organizations. If such a promising prospect indeed comes to pass, then the final outcome of political globalization might well be the emergence of a *cosmopolitan democracy* that would constitute the basis for a plurality of identities flourishing within a structure of mutual toleration and accountability (see Figure E).

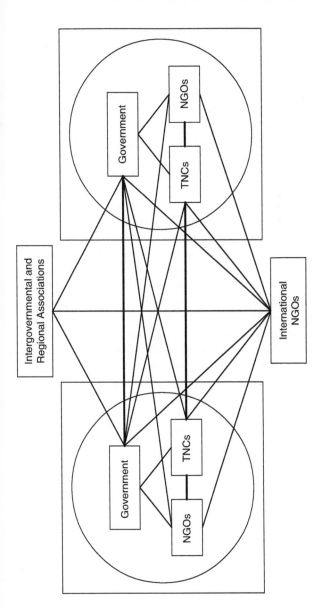

E. Incipient global governance: a network of interrelated power centres.

According to David Held, one of the chief academic proponents of this view, such a cosmopolitan democracy of the future would contain the following features:

1. A global parliament connected to regions, states, and localities;
2. A new charter of rights and duties locked into different domains of political, social, and economic power;
3. The formal separation of political and economic interests;
4. An interconnected global legal system with mechanisms of enforcement from the local to the global.

A number of less optimistic commentators have challenged Held's idea that political globalization is moving in the direction of cosmopolitan democracy, especially in light of the current populist backlash against globalization. Most criticisms of Held's benign world vision boil down to the charge that it represents an abstract idealism that fails to engage enduring political tensions on the national level of public policy such as the clashing immigration perspectives within the EU. Global governance sceptics have also expressed the suspicion that the proponents of cosmopolitan democracy have not considered in sufficient detail its cultural feasibility. In other words, the worldwide intensification of cultural interactions makes the possibility of political resistance and opposition just as real as the benign vision of mutual accommodation and tolerance of differences. To follow up on this cultural dimension of globalization, let us turn to Chapter 5.

Chapter 5
The cultural dimension of globalization

As this book's opening discussion of Matt Stopera's lost iPhone demonstrates, even a *very short* introduction to globalization would be woefully inadequate without an examination of its cultural dimension. *Cultural globalization* refers to the intensification and expansion of cultural flows across the globe. Obviously, *culture* is a very broad concept. Referring to patterns of meaning and ways of life, it is frequently used to describe the whole of human experience. In order to avoid the ensuing danger of overgeneralization, it is important to make analytical distinctions between various aspects of social life. For example, we associate the adjective 'economic' with the production, exchange, and consumption of commodities. If we are discussing the 'political', we mean practices related to the generation and distribution of power in societies. If we are talking about the 'cultural', we are concerned with the symbolic construction, articulation, and dissemination of meaning. Given that language, music, and images constitute the major forms of symbolic expression, they assume special significance for the dynamics of cultural interactions.

The exploding network of cultural interconnections in the last decades has led some commentators to suggest that such practices lie at the very heart of contemporary globalization. Yet, cultural globalization did not start with the worldwide dissemination of rock ' n' roll, Coca-Cola, or football. As noted in Chapter 2, expansive civilizational exchanges are much older than modernity. Still, both the volume and extent of cultural transmissions in the 21st century have far exceeded those of earlier times. Turbocharged by the digital social media and our proliferating mobile digital devices, the dominant symbolic systems of meaning of our global age—such as individualism, consumerism, and various religious discourses—circulate more freely and widely than ever before. As images and ideas can be more easily and rapidly transmitted from one place to another, they profoundly impact the way people experience their everyday lives. As we noted in our lost cell phone story in Chapter 1, cultural practices have escaped the prison of fixed localities such as town and nation, eventually acquiring new *glocal* meanings in interaction with dominant global themes.

The thematic landscape traversed by scholars of cultural globalization is vast and the questions they raise are too numerous to be fleshed out in this short introduction. Rather than offering a long laundry list of relevant topics, this chapter will focus on three important themes: the tension between sameness and difference in the emerging global culture; the crucial role of transnational media corporations in disseminating popular culture; and the globalization of languages.

Global culture: sameness or difference?

Does globalization make people around the world more alike or more different? This is the question most frequently raised in discussions on the subject of cultural globalization. A group of commentators we might call *pessimistic globalizers* argue in favour of the former. They suggest that we are not moving towards a cultural rainbow that reflects the diversity of the world's existing populations. Rather, we are witnessing the rise of an increasingly homogenized popular culture underwritten by a Western 'culture industry' based in New York, Hollywood, London, Paris, and

Milan. As evidence for their interpretation, these commentators point to Amazonian Indians wearing Nike sneakers; denizens of the Southern Sahara purchasing Yankees baseball caps; and Palestinian youths proudly displaying their Golden State Warriors basketball singlets in downtown Ramallah. This portrayal of globalization as a ruthless homogenizing force spreading the logic of Anglo-American capitalism and Western values at the expense of local and national cultures has become very influential. It has appeared as the spectre of *Americanization* stalking vulnerable regions of the world. Although there have been serious attempts by some countries to resist what is often referred to as 'cultural imperialism'—for example, a ban on satellite dishes in Iran, and the French imposition of tariffs and quotas on imported films and television programmes—the spread of American popular culture seems to be unstoppable.

But these manifestations of sameness are also evident inside the dominant countries of the global North. American sociologist George Ritzer coined the term *McDonaldization* to describe the wide-ranging sociocultural processes by which the principles of the fast-food restaurant are coming to dominate more and more sectors of American society as well as the rest of the world. On the surface, these principles appear to be rational in their attempts to offer efficient and predictable ways of serving people's needs.

However, looking behind the façade of repetitive TV commercials that claim to 'love to see you smile', we can identify a number of serious problems. For one, the generally low nutritional value of fast-food meals—and particularly their high fat content—has been implicated in the rise of serious health problems such as heart disease, diabetes, cancer, and juvenile obesity (see Table 2). Moreover, the idea that impersonal, routine operations of 'rational' fast-service establishments actually apply to the rest of the world undermines expressions of *cultural diversity*. In the long run, the McDonaldization of the world amounts to the imposition of uniform standards that eclipse human creativity and

Table 2. The American way of life

Average daily time Americans spend watching TV (in minutes in 2019)	215
Average daily time Americans spend communicating face to face (in minutes in 2014)	46
Average daily time Americans spend on mobile devices (in minutes in 2019)	223
Number of advertisements, logos, and labels seen by the average American every day (2013)	16,000
Percentage of adult Americans who are obese (2016)	39.6%
Average annual intake of meat per person in the USA vs India (in kg in 2018)	101 vs 4
Average annual meat intake per person in USA equals how many hamburgers (2018)	800
Average number of different cows in a single fast-food hamburger patty (2017)	100+
CO_2 produced to make a single hamburger (in kg in 2017)	4
Annual CO_2 output created by the US production of hamburgers (in metric tonnes in 2017)	195,750,000
Netherlands' annual CO_2 output (in metric tonnes in 2017)	174,770,000
Number of cars registered in the USA (in millions in 2019)	281
Amount of rubbish produced by Americans (in million tonnes in 2015)	262
Total mass of living humans on Earth (in million tonnes in 2017)	287
Percentage of Americans who believe that God created humans in their present form less than 10,000 years ago (2017)	38%
Total US population (in millions in 2018) vs number of civilian-held firearms in the USA (in millions in 2018)	329 vs 393

Percentage of civilian-held firearms in the USA as share of the worldwide total of firearms (2018)	46%
Annual number of people killed by firearms in the USA vs Japan (2017)	39,773 vs 3

Sources: Leopold Center for Sustainable Agriculture, 2003, 'Checking the food odometer: Comparing food miles for local versus conventional produce sales to Iowa institutions':<https://lib.dr.iastate.edu/leopold_pubspapers/130/; Centre for Disease Control and Prevention: <http://www.cdc.gov/obesity/data/adult.html>; Jamais Cascio, The Cheeseburger Footprint, 2012: <http://www.openthefuture.com/cheeseburger_CF.html>; Statista: <http://www.statista.com/statistics/271380/average-tv-viewing-time-in-north-america/>; Bureau of Labor Statistics, 2012: <http://www.bls.gov/news.release/atus.nr0.htm>; Dharma Singh Khalsa, Brain Longevity, Grand Central Publishing, p. 29; Norman Herr, The Sourcebook for Teaching Science, 2012:<http://www.csun.edu/science/health/docs/tv&health.html>; Statista: <http://www.statista.com/statistics/183505/number-of-vehicles-in-the-united-states-since-1990/>; Statista: <http://www.statista.com/statistics/189527/daily-time-spent-on-socializing-and-communicating-in-the-us- since-2009/>; Gallup Poll, Evolution, Creationism, Intelligent Design, 2012:<http://www.gallup.com/poll/21814/evolution-creationism-intelligent-design.aspx>; TV Week:<http://www.tvweek.com/tvbizwire/2014/05/how-many-minutes-of-commercial/>; Environmental Protection Agency: <https://www.epa.gov/smm/advancing-sustainable-materials-management-facts-and-figures>; Michael Marshall, 'Humanity weighs in at 287 million tonnes', 2012:<http://www.newscientist.com/article/dn21945-humanity-weighs-in-at-287-million-tonnes.html>

dehumanize social relations. In order to expand markets and make more profit, global capitalists are developing homogeneous global products targeting especially the young and wealthy throughout the world, as well as turning children into avid consumers from a very early age. Thus, global consumerism becomes an increasingly soulless and unethical cultural framework.

While *optimistic globalizers* agree with their pessimistic colleagues that cultural globalization generates more sameness, they nonetheless consider this pattern of sameness to be a good thing. For example, the American social theorist Francis Fukuyama explicitly welcomes the global spread of Anglo-American values and lifestyles, equating the Americanization of the world with the desirable expansion of democracy and free markets (see Figure 11). But optimistic globalizers do not just come in the form of American nationalists who apply the old national theme of *manifest destiny* to the global arena. Still, some representatives

11. Jihad vs McWorld: selling fast food in Indonesia.

of this camp consider themselves staunch cosmopolitans who celebrate social media and the latest digital devices as the harbinger of a homogenized techno-culture. Others are unabashed free-market enthusiasts who embrace the values of global consumer capitalism.

While acknowledging globalization's homogenization dynamic, we should also note its tendencies towards cultural diversification and hybridization. It is one thing to acknowledge the existence of powerful sameness tendencies in the world, but it is quite another to assert that most cultural diversity existing on our planet is destined to vanish. In fact, several influential commentators offer a contrary assessment that links globalization to multiplying forms of cultural expression. Sociologist Roland Robertson, for example, contends that global cultural flows often reinvigorate local cultural niches. The result is often visible in the proliferation of culturally specific festivals and large urban parades celebrating marginalized values represented by such groups as the GLBTQ community.

Hence, rather than being totally obliterated by the Western consumerist forces of sameness, local difference and particularity still play an important role in creating unique cultural constellations. Arguing that cultural globalization always takes place in local contexts, Global Studies scholars like Jan Nederveen Pieterse reject the cultural homogenization thesis and speak instead of *glocalization*—a complex dynamic involving the interaction of the global and local we explored in the example of the stolen iPhone in Chapter 1. The resulting expressions of *hybridity* cannot be reduced to clear-cut manifestations of 'sameness' or 'difference'. Such processes of *cultural hybridization* have become most visible in fashion, music, dance, film, food, sports, and language.

But the respective arguments of optimistic and pessimistic globalizers are not necessarily incompatible. The contemporary experience of living and acting across cultural borders often means both the loss of traditional meanings and the creation of new symbolic expressions. Reconstructed feelings of belonging coexist in uneasy tension with a sense of placelessness. Other commentators like the late sociologist Ulrich Beck have pointed to the rapid increase of *place-bigamists*—people whose enhanced mobility allows them to feel at home in more than just one place. Seen from this perspective, it appears that a homogenized form of modernity is actually giving way to a new *postmodern* framework characterized by a less stable sense of identity, place, meaning, and knowledge.

Given the complexity of global cultural flows, one would actually expect to see uneven and contradictory effects. In certain contexts, these flows might change traditional manifestations of national identity in the direction of a popular culture characterized by sameness; in others they might foster new expressions of cultural particularism; in still others they might encourage forms of cultural hybridity. Those commentators who summarily denounce the homogenizing effects of Americanization must not forget that hardly any society in our globalizing world possesses an 'authentic', self-contained culture. In fact, cultural hybridity seems to be ubiquitous in today's globalizing world. Think, for example, of the emotional exuberance of Bollywood pop songs, the intricacy of several variations of Hawaiian pidgin, the culinary delights of Cuban-Chinese cuisine. Finally, those who applaud the spread of consumerist capitalism also need to pay attention to its negative consequences, such as the dramatic decline of traditional communal folkways as well as the commodification of society and nature.

The role of the media

To a large extent, the global cultural flows of our time are generated and directed by sprawling media empires that rely on powerful communication technologies to spread their message. *Media* covers a wide variety of streams—advertising, broadcasting and networking, news, print and publication, digital, recording, and motion pictures. Saturating global cultural reality with formulaic TV shows and mindless advertisements, these corporations increasingly shape people's identities and the structure of desires around the world. The rise of the global imaginary is inextricably connected to the rise of the global media. During the last two decades, a small group of gigantic TNCs have come to dominate the global market for entertainment, news, television, and film. In 2019, the eight largest media conglomerates—Comcast, Disney, Alphabet, Charter Communications, AT&T, Twenty-First Century Fox, Thomson Reuters, and CBS News Corporation—accounted for more than two-thirds of the $2.5 trillion in annual worldwide revenues generated by the global telecommunications industry.

As recently as twenty years ago, many of today's giant dominant corporations did not exist in their present form as all-encompassing media companies. Today, most media analysts concede that the emergence of a global commercial-media market amounts to the creation of a global oligopoly similar to that of the oil and automotive industries in the early part of the 20th century. The crucial cultural innovators of earlier decades—small, independent record labels, radio stations, movie theatres, newspapers, and book publishers—have become virtually extinct as they have found themselves incapable of competing with today's media giants.

The commercial values disseminated by transnational media enterprises not only secure the undisputed cultural hegemony of popular culture, but also can lead to the depoliticization of social reality and the weakening of civic bonds. One of the most glaring developments of the last two decades has been the transformation of news broadcasts and educational programmes into shallow entertainment shows—many of them ironically touted as 'reality shows' such as *The Apprentice*, which ran in the USA on NBC across fourteen seasons and served as the publicity foundation for Donald Trump's successful 2016 presidential campaign. Given that news is less than half as profitable as entertainment, media firms are increasingly tempted to pursue higher profits by ignoring journalism's much vaunted separation of newsroom practices and business decisions. Partnerships and alliances between news and entertainment companies are fast becoming the norm, making it more common for publishing executives to press journalists to cooperate with their newspapers' business operations. A sustained attack on the professional autonomy of journalists, which accuses them of spreading 'fake news', is, therefore, also part of cultural globalization.

The globalization of languages

One direct method of measuring and evaluating cultural changes brought about by globalization is to study the shifting global patterns of language use. The globalization of languages can be viewed as a process by which some languages are increasingly used in international communication while others lose their prominence and even disappear for lack of speakers. Researchers at the Globalization Research Center at the University of Hawai'i have identified five key variables that influence the globalization of languages:

1. *Number of languages:* The declining number of languages in different parts of the world points to the strengthening of homogenizing cultural forces.
2. *Movements of people:* People carry their languages with them when they migrate and travel. Migration patterns affect the spread of languages.
3. *Foreign language learning and tourism:* Foreign language learning and tourism facilitate the spread of languages beyond national or cultural boundaries.
4. *Internet languages:* The Internet has become a global medium for instant communication and quick access to information. Language use on the Internet is a key factor in the analysis of the dominance and variety of languages in international communication.
5. *International scientific publications:* International scientific publications, both online and print, contain the languages of global intellectual discourse, thus critically impacting intellectual communities involved in the production, reproduction, and circulation of knowledge around the world.

Given these highly complex interactions, research in this area frequently yields contradictory conclusions. Unable to reach a general agreement, experts in the field have developed several different hypotheses. One model posits a clear correlation between the growing global significance of a few languages—particularly English, Chinese, and Spanish—and the declining number of other languages around the world. Another model suggests that the globalization of language does not necessarily mean that our descendants are destined to utilize only a few tongues. Still another thesis emphasizes the power of the Anglo-American culture industry to make English—or what some commentators call 'Globish'—*the* global lingua franca of the 21st century.

Table 3. The declining number of languages around the world, 1500–2000

Continents	Early 16th Century	Early 17th Century	Early 18th Century	Early 19th Century	Early 20th Century	Late 20th Century
Americas	2,175	2,025	1,800	1,500	1,125	1,005
Africa	4,350	4,050	3,600	3,000	2,250	2,011
Europe	435	405	360	300	225	201
Asia	4,785	4,455	3,960	3,300	2,475	2,212
Pacific	2,755	2,565	2,280	1,900	1,425	1,274
World	14,500	13,500	12,000	10,000	7,500	6,703

Source: Globalization Research Center at the University of Hawai'i-Mānoa.

To be sure, the rising significance of the English language has a long history, reaching back to the birth of British colonialism in the late 16th century. At that time, only approximately 7 million people used English as their mother tongue. By the 1990s, this number had swollen to over 350 million native speakers, with 400 million more using English as a second language. Almost half of the world's growing population of foreign students is enrolled at institutions in Anglo-American countries. In 2018, more than 54 per cent of the content posted at the top 100 million websites on the World Wide Web was in English; only 1.7 per cent was in Chinese.

At the same time, however, the number of spoken languages in the world has dropped from about 14,500 in 1500 to about 6,700 in 2000 (see Table 3). By the end of the second decade of the 21st century, this number had dropped to 6,300, with 2,000 of those languages spoken by fewer than 1,000 people. Given the current rate of decline, some linguists predict that 50–90 per cent of the currently existing languages will have disappeared by the end of the 21st century. But the world's languages are not the only entities threatened with extinction. The spread of consumerist values and materialist lifestyles has endangered the ecological health of our planet as well. It is to this crucial ecological dimension of globalization we now must turn.

Chapter 6
The ecological dimension of globalization

Although we have examined the economic, political, and cultural aspects of globalization separately, it is important to remember that each of these dimensions impacts on and has consequences for the other domains. Nowhere is this more clearly demonstrated than in the ecological dimension of globalization. In recent years, global environmental issues such as global climate change and transboundary pollution have received enormous attention from research institutes, the media, politicians, economists, and the public in general. Unsustainable forms of *ecological globalization* are now recognized as threatening all life on our planet. The worldwide impacts of natural and man-made disasters—such as the horrifying 1986 nuclear plant accidents at Chernobyl, Ukraine, and Fukushima, Japan, in 2011, or the massive 2010 Deepwater Horizon oil spill in the Gulf of Mexico—clearly show that the formidable environmental problems of our time can only be tackled by a global alliance of states and civil society actors.

In the 21st century, it has become virtually impossible to ignore the fact that people everywhere on our planet are inextricably linked to each other through the air they breathe, the climate they depend upon, the food they eat, and the water they drink. In spite of this obvious lesson of interdependence, our planet's ecosystems are subjected to continuous human assault in order to maintain wasteful lifestyles. Indeed, cultural values greatly influence how people view their natural environment. For example, cultures steeped in Taoist, Buddhist, and various animist religions often emphasize the interdependence of all living beings—even if their adapted capitalist practices do not always live up to their cultural imperative of maintaining a delicate balance between human wants and ecological needs. Judaeo-Christian humanism contains deeply dualistic values that put humans in control of nature. In Western modernity, the environment has thus come to be considered as a 'resource' to be used instrumentally to fulfil human needs and desires. Consider, for example, the clear-cutting of rainforests around the world in the name of 'harvesting resources'. It threatens the livelihood and cultures of indigenous people, not to speak of the countless animal and plant species that have been wiped out merely to serve oversized human demands.

As we noted in Chapter 5, the most extreme manifestation of this *anthropocentric* paradigm is reflected in the dominant values and beliefs of consumerism. The capitalist culture industry seeks to convince its global audience that the meaning and chief value of life can be found in the limitless accumulation of material goods. Recently, researchers capable of linking natural and social history have suggested that the damaging impact of human activity on our planet justifies the naming of a new current geological period: the *Anthropocene*—the age when human activity has become the dominant influence on Earth's climate and environment.

In the last few decades, the scale, speed, and depth of Earth's ecological decline have been unprecedented. Consider, for example some of the most dangerous manifestations of the globalization of environmental degradation depicted in Figure F.

Two major concerns relate to still uncontrolled population growth in parts of the global South and the lavish consumption patterns in the global North. Since farming economies first came into existence about 480 generations ago, the world population has exploded a thousand-fold to reach nearly 7.7 billion in 2019.

F. **Major manifestations and consequences of global environmental degradation.**

Half of this increase has occurred in the last thirty years. With the possible exception of rats and mice, humans are now the most numerous mammals on earth. Vastly increased demands for food, timber, and fibre have put severe pressure on the planet's ecosystems.

Large areas of the Earth's surface, especially in arid and semi-arid regions, have been used for agricultural production for millennia, yielding crops for ever-increasing numbers of people. Concerns about the relationship between population growth and environmental degradation are frequently focused rather narrowly on aggregate population levels. Yet, the global impact of humans on the environment is as much a function of per capita consumption as it is of overall population size (see Table 4). For example, the United States comprises only 6 per cent of the

Table 4. Annual consumption patterns (per capita) in selected countries, 2015–2019

	Annual oil consumption per capita (in litres)	Automobiles per 1,000 people	Annual meat consumption per capita (in kg)	Annual withdrawal of fresh water per capita (in cubic metres)
USA	3,526	811	116	1,582
South Korea	2,658	411	63	498
Sweden	1,724	536	82	565
Brazil	900	350	97	415
Egypt	532	62	31	847
China	476	173	62	442
Chad	11	6	12	24

Sources: Oil: World by Map, <http://world.bymap.org/OilConsumption.html>; Cars: Wikipedia, <https://en.wikipedia.org/wiki/List_of_countries_by_vehicles_per_capita>; Meat: Our World in Data, <https://ourworldindata.org/meat-and-seafood-production-consumption>; Water: Statista, < https://www.statista.com/statistics/263156/water-consumption-in-selected-countries/> and UN FAO Aquastats, <http://www.fao.org/nr/water/aquastat/countries_regions/>.

world's population, yet it consumes 30–40 per cent of our planet's natural resources. Together, regional overconsumption and uncontrolled population growth present a serious problem to the health of our planet. Unless we are willing to rethink the relentless drive for profits-at-all-cost that sustains these ominous dynamics, the health of Mother Earth is likely to deteriorate further.

Some of the effects of overconsumption and population growth are painfully obvious in the recurrent food crises plaguing vast regions of our planet. Large-scale food riots in Haiti, Indonesia, the Philippines, China, and Cameroon in recent years highlight increasing limitations on access to food in part as a result of environmental problems such as drought. Other factors include rising oil prices (which affect the cost of transportation of food), diversion of food staples such as corn into production of biofuels in efforts to reduce reliance on petroleum, and unequal access to resources across developed and developing countries. The problem of adequate food supply for so many people highlights the interconnections between political, economic, and ecological problems that are accentuated by the process of globalization.

Another significant ecological problem associated with population increases and the globalization of environmental degradation is the worldwide *reduction of biodiversity*. Seven out of ten biologists today believe that the world is now in the midst of the fastest mass extinction of living species in the 4.5-billion-year history of the planet. According to recent OECD reports, two-thirds of the world's farmlands have been rated as 'somewhat degraded' and one-third have been marked as 'strongly degraded'. Half the world's wetlands have already been destroyed, and the biodiversity of freshwater ecosystems is under serious threat. Three-quarters of worldwide genetic diversity in agricultural crop and animal breeds has been lost since 1900. Some experts fear that up to 50 per cent of all plant and animal species—most of them in the global South—will disappear by the end of this century. Hence, many environmentalists argue that biodiversity should be treated as a planetary asset and held in trust for the benefit of future generations.

Some of the measures currently undertaken to safeguard biodiversity include the creation of hundreds of *gene banks* located in over a hundred countries around the world. One of the most spectacular of these banks is the Svalbard Global Seed Vault buried in permafrost in a mountain on the Arctic island of Spitzbergen. Officially opened in 2008, this 'Doomsday Vault' was funded by The Global Crop Diversity Trust (financed by international donors like the Gates and Rockefeller Foundations) and specially designed to store back-up copies of the seeds of the world's major food crops at −18°C. Operating like a safety deposit box in a bank, the Global Seed Vault is free of charge to public and private depositors and kept safe by the Norwegian government. But it is doubtful that such laudable back-up measures are sufficient to reverse the escalating loss of biodiversity brought about by humanity's ecological footprint.

Transboundary pollution represents another grave danger to our collective survival. The release of vast amounts of synthetic chemicals into the air and water has created conditions for human and animal life that are outside previous limits of biological experience. For example, chlorofluorocarbons (CFCs) were used in the second half of the 20th century as non-flammable refrigerants, industrial solvents, foaming agents, and aerosol propellants. In the mid-1970s, researchers noted that the unregulated release of CFCs into the air seemed to be depleting Earth's protective ozone layer. A decade later, the discovery of large 'ozone holes' over Tasmania, New Zealand, and large parts of the Antarctic finally resulted in a coordinated international effort to phase out production of CFCs and other ozone-depleting substances. Scientists have warned that the risk of damage to the world's ozone layer has increased as a result of more frequent and severe storms and other extreme weather events associated with global climate change. Other forms of transboundary pollution include industrial emissions of sulphur and nitrogen oxides. Returning to the ground in the form of acid rain, these chemicals damage forests, soils, and freshwater ecosystems. Current acid deposits in northern Europe and parts of North America are far higher than the tolerable range suggested by environmental agencies.

Finally, the ominous phenomenon of *human-induced climate change* has emerged as *the* major focus of domestic and intergovernmental policy as well as grass roots activism. Brought to public attention by former US Vice President Al Gore in the 2000s through his award-winning documentary *An Inconvenient Truth*—as well as the production of numerous scientific reports outlining the dire consequences of unchecked global warming—climate change is clearly one of the top global problems facing humanity today.

But perhaps the most influential recent attempt to raise people's consciousness about the dangers of global climate change came from an unexpected quarter: the Vatican in Rome. In September 2015, Pope Francis I stood before the UN General Assembly and issued a radical call for the world to address global warming (see Figure 12). Connecting the issue of climate change to the wider pursuit of equality, security, and social justice, the pontiff went so far as to send his shoes to the 2015 UNIPCC Climate Summit in Paris, to be displayed at the city's Place de la République together with thousands of shoes of other climate-change protesters as a public symbol to curb carbon emissions (see Box 9).

The consequences of worldwide climate change, especially global warming, could be catastrophic. A large number of scientists are calling for concerted action by governments to curb greenhouse gas emissions. Indeed, global warming represents a grim example of the decisive shift in both the intensity and extent of contemporary environmental problems. The rapid build-up of gas emissions, including carbon dioxide, methane, nitrous and sulphur oxides, and CFCs, in our planet's atmosphere has greatly

12. Pope Francis I addresses the UN General Assembly on climate change, 25 September 2015.

Box 9. Pope Francis's climate appeal

'I urgently appeal, then, for a new dialogue about how we are shaping the future of our planet. We need a conversation which includes everyone, since the environmental challenge we are undergoing, and its human roots, concern and affect us all. The worldwide ecological movement has already made considerable progress and led to the establishment of numerous organizations committed to raising awareness of these challenges. Regrettably, many efforts to seek concrete solutions to the environmental crisis have proved ineffective, not only because of powerful opposition but also because of a more general lack of interest. Obstructionist attitudes, even on the part of believers, can range from denial of the problem to indifference, nonchalant resignation or blind confidence in technical solutions. We require a new and universal solidarity.'

enhanced Earth's capacity to trap heat. The resulting *greenhouse effect* is responsible for raising average temperatures worldwide (see Figure 13).

The precise effects of global warming are difficult to calculate. According to a 2018 report by the United Nations Intergovernmental Panel on Climate Change (IPCC), the world reached 1°C global warming above pre-industrial levels in 2017. It is now heading towards 1.5°C within a decade or so. The *high confidence* range predicted for this threshold is between 2030 and 2052. At more than 2°C global warming, it has been suggested that the world will descend towards ecological chaos, with the most severe impacts hitting the equatorial regions. To give some sense of the difference between these two apparently close thresholds: at 1.5°C, the IPCC estimates that around 80 per cent of coral reefs will be gone; at 2°C, they will be 99 per cent destroyed. Even today, higher temperatures are already worsening many kinds of extreme weather events, including storms, wildfires, floods, and droughts. Nine of the ten warmest years have occurred since 2005, with the last five years comprising the five

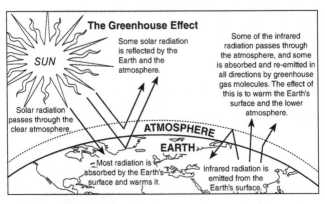

13. The greenhouse effect.

hottest. Disasters caused by global climate change not only endanger human lives, but cause trillions of dollars of damage.

These significant increases in global temperatures have also led to meltdowns of large chunks of the world's major ice reserves. The polar ice caps have melted faster in the last twenty years than in the last 10,000. The large Greenland ice sheet is shrinking the fastest, and its complete melting would result in a global rise of sea levels of up to 22 feet. However, even a much smaller sea level rise would spell doom for many coastal regions around the world. The small Pacific island nations of Tuvalu and Kiribati, for example, would disappear. Large coastal cities such as Tokyo, New York, London, and Sydney would lose significant chunks of their urban landscapes.

But sea level and water temperature rise as a result of global warming are not the only serious problems threatening the health of our planet's oceans. Overfishing, the loss of coral reefs, coastal pollution, acidification, mega-oil spills, and illegal dumping of hazardous wastes have had a devastating impact on Earth's marine environments. Consider, for example, the *Great Pacific Garbage Patch*—a gigantic floating mass of often toxic, non-biodegradable plastics and chemical sludge twice the size of Texas that circulates permanently in the powerful currents of the Northern Pacific Ocean.

Or, perhaps even more horrifying, take the huge floating debris field generated by the devastating Japanese earthquake and tsunami of March 2011 that killed more than 15,000 people across Japan. The disaster caused the partial destruction of the Fukushima Daiichi nuclear plant, in the process allowing the escape of harmful radioactive particles into air and water. Stretching for nearly 2,000 miles and still containing 1.5 million tonnes of detritus (3.5 million tonnes have already sunk), this debris field crossed the Pacific in only fifteen months. It deposited on North America's Pacific coast massive amounts of partially toxic materials such as wall insulation, oil and gas canisters, car tyres, fishing nets, and Styrofoam buoys. Heavier items are drifting underwater and might wash up in years to come.

The central feature of all these potentially disastrous environmental problems is that they are *glocal*, thus making them serious problems for all sentient beings inhabiting our magnificent blue planet. The dark side of unchecked environmental glocalization became especially visible in the estimated 87,000 wildfires that raged in the Amazon region of Brazil in the summer of 2019. Encouraged by the anti-ecological views of the country's newly elected populist President Jair Bolsonaro, scores of Brazilian ranchers and farmers had intentionally set many of those fires to clear heavily forested land for agricultural purposes. As French President Emmanuel Macron pointed out, these local burnings had serious global consequences. After all, the Amazonian rainforests serve as the world's 'lungs' by producing 20 per cent of our planet's oxygen. Indeed, transboundary pollution, global warming, climate change, and species extinction are challenges that cannot be contained within national or even regional borders. They do not have isolated causes and effects, for they are caused by aggregate collective human actions and thus require a coordinated global response.

To be sure, ecological problems aggravated by globalization also have significant economic ramifications. Although these effects will be more significant for less developed countries than for rich countries, they will nonetheless affect all people and all nations. Poor countries do not have the necessary infrastructure or income to adapt to the unavoidable climate changes that will occur because of carbon emissions already in the earth's atmosphere. As we noted, developing regions are already warmer on average than most developed countries and consequently suffer from a high degree of variability in rainfall. To make matters worse, less developed countries are also heavily dependent on agriculture for the majority of their income. Since agriculture is the most climate sensitive of all economic sectors, developing nations will be more adversely affected by climate change than developed countries.

Further consequences of this vicious circle include increased illnesses, escalating death rates, and crumbling infrastructure. The cost of living will continue to rise, leaving poor households and communities unable to save for future emergencies. Recent scientific reviews like the Stern Report explicitly link the problem of climate change to development and aid provision in poor countries. They will require assistance from the developed world if they are to adapt and survive climate change. Thus, climate change and global warming are not merely environmental or scientific issues. They are economic, political, cultural, but, above all, ethical issues that have been expanded and intensified by the process of globalization.

There has been much debate in public and academic circles about the severity of climate change and the best ways for the global community to respond to it. As can be gleaned from the list of major global environmental treaties, international discussion on the issue of global warming and environmental degradation has been occurring for over thirty years. Yet, while much has been written and spoken about this issue, few coordinated measures have been implemented. Most international environmental treaties still lack effective enforcement mechanisms.

For the most part, political efforts in favour of immediate change have been limited. In December 2015, however, the UN Framework Convention on Climate Change summit held in Paris, France, proved to be a turning point for action to limit climate change with an expressed objective to move to a zero carbon world within the foreseeable future. Uniting all of the world's nations in a single agreement on tackling climate change for the first time in history, the *Paris global climate deal* comprised a number of key elements (see Table 5).

Table 5. Major global environmental treaties/conferences, 1972–2015

Name of Treaty/Conference	Coverage/protection	Date
UNESCO-World Heritage, Paris	Cultural and natural heritage	1972
UNEP Conference, Stockholm	General environment	1972
CITES, Washington, DC	Endangered species	1973
Marine pollution treaty, London	Marine pollution from ships	1978
UN Convention on Law of the Sea	Marine species, pollution	1982
Vienna Protocol	Ozone layer	1985
Montreal Protocol	Ozone layer	1987
Basel Convention	Hazardous wastes	1989
UN 'Rio Summit' on Environmental Climate Change	Biodiversity	1992
Jakarta Mandate	Marine and coastal diversity	1995
Kyoto Protocol	Global warming	1997
Rotterdam Convention	Industrial pollution	1998
Johannesburg World Summit	Ecological sustainability, pollution	2002
Bali Action Plan	Global warming	2007
UN Copenhagen Climate Summit	Global warming	2009
UN Cancun Climate Summit	Global warming	2010
UN Durban Climate Summit	Global warming	2011
UN Rio + 20	Sustainable development	2012
UN Paris Climate Summit	Climate change	2015

First, the parties committed themselves to arresting the rise of global temperatures. Second, they pledged to limit the amount of greenhouse gases emitted by human activity to the same levels that trees, soil, and oceans can absorb naturally, beginning at some point between 2050 and 2100. Third, countries agreed to review each other's contribution to cutting emissions every five years so as to scale up the challenge. Finally, rich countries promised to help poorer nations by providing 'climate finance' geared toward climate change adaptation and hastening the switch to renewable energy. After all, poor countries have not been responsible for the production of most of the greenhouse gases that have caused the current problem. Thus, the Paris climate deal establishes that the major burden for limiting the production of greenhouse gases should fall on the developed world—at least until developing countries have pulled their populations out of poverty.

While the final signing of the Paris Agreement in 2016 constituted an important milestone in the global struggle for environmental sustainability, it nonetheless represented only the first step on the long road to a zero carbon world powered by non-fossil energy sources such as solar, wind, and wave. But even this first major step in the direction of global environmental sustainability was severely undermined when the Trump administration announced in June 2017 that it was withdrawing from the Paris Agreement, alleging that it 'damaged' the US economy. Instead, the government submitted its 'America's First Energy Plan', which presents a reversal of the Obama administration's commitment to renewable energy. It also rolled back environmental regulations and emission standards, in addition to calling for more oil drilling—even in some National Parks and previously protected offshore locations. Finally, the new policy document articulated a clear commitment to support the fossil fuels industry, including a return to massive coal mining. The US President has repeatedly called global climate change a 'Chinese hoax' and refuses to commit his country to a necessary reduction of carbon emissions.

Table 6. The top ten carbon dioxide emitters, 2019

Country	Total emissions (million tonnes of CO_2)	Per capita emissions (tonnes per capita)
People's Republic of China	9,839	6.9
United States of America	5,269	16.1
India	2,467	1.8
Russian Federation	1,693	11.7
Japan	1,205	9.4
Germany	799	9.6
Islamic Republic of Iran	672	8.1
Saudi Arabia	635	18.6
South Korea	616	12.0
Canada	573	15.2
Global total	36,153	4.7

Source: World Economic Forum, <https://www.weforum.org/agenda/2019/06/chart-of-the-day-these-countries-create-most-of-the-world-s-co2-emissions/>

Yet, inaction on climate change today will have more dire consequences for economic growth tomorrow (see Tables 6 and 7).

Indeed, the debate over climate change serves as another instructive example for how the major dimensions of globalization intersect. In this case, political and cultural globalization simply has not kept up with the ecological demands of our planet. But time is of the essence. Some leading scientists believe that a further decade or two of slow or no action would make it too late to reverse the disastrous course of climate change and ecological

Table 7. Long-term global CO_2 emissions, 1750–2020

Year	Million metric tonnes of carbon
1750	3
1800	8
1850	54
1900	534
1950	1,630
2000	23,650
2020	37,000

Source: Our World in Data, <https://ourworldindata.org/co2-and-other-greenhouse-gas-emissions>.

degradation. Confronted with the ill health of our Mother Earth at the beginning of the third decade of the 21st century, it has become abundantly clear to many people that the contemporary phase of globalization has been the most environmentally destructive period in human history. It remains to be seen, however, whether the growing recognition of the ecological limits of our planet will translate swiftly into profound new forms of political cooperation across borders. As we shall discuss in Chapter 7, much depends on the outcome of the current ideological struggle over the meaning and direction of globalization.

Chapter 7
Ideological confrontations over globalization

Like all social processes, globalization operates in an *ideological* dimension filled with potent narratives about the phenomenon itself—such as the heated public debate over whether globalization should be seen as 'good' or 'bad'. *Ideologies* are powerful systems of widely shared ideas and patterned beliefs that are accepted as truth by significant groups in society. Serving as shared mental maps, they offer people a more or less coherent picture of the world not only as it is, but also how it ought to be. In doing so, ideologies help organize the tremendous complexity of human experiences into fairly simple claims that serve as guide and compass for social and political action. These claims are employed by social elites to legitimize their interests and to defend or challenge existing power structures. Thus, ideologies connect theory and practice by orienting and organizing human action.

Contrary to the utopian claim of an 'end of ideology' that gained much popularity at the end of the Cold War, the early 21st century has witnessed fierce *ideological confrontations* between various forms of 'globalism'. *Market globalism* is the dominant ideology that seeks to endow 'globalization' with free-market norms and neoliberal meanings. Contesting it from the political Left, *justice globalism* constructs an alternative vision of globalization based on egalitarian ideals of global solidarity and distributive justice. From the political Right, *religious globalism* struggles against both market globalism and justice globalism as it seeks to mobilize a religious community imagined in global terms. In spite of their considerable differences, however, the three globalisms discussed in this chapter share an important function: they translate the rising global imaginary—deep-seated modes of imagining community as a global social whole—into competing political programmes and agendas.

Over the last few years, this global battle of ideas has been joined by powerful voices of *anti-globalization* that cling to the national imaginary of the past. *Antiglobalist populists* and *economic protectionists* such as Donald Trump (Figure 14) in the USA, Marine Le Pen in France, and Nigel Farage in the UK, have made much headway in challenging the ideological dominance of market globalism. Their political vision reflects their fierce opposition to the transnational dynamics at the core of globalization. Let us now examine each of these influential ideologies in turn.

14. US President Donald J. Trump addressing the UN General Assembly, 25 September 2018.

Market globalism

The world's dominant political ideology since the early 1990s, market globalism has been codified and disseminated worldwide by global power elites that include corporate managers, executives of large transnational corporations, corporate lobbyists, influential journalists and public-relations specialists, public intellectuals, celebrities and entertainers, state bureaucrats, and politicians. Serving as the chief advocates of market globalism, these individuals saturate the public discourse with neoliberal images of a consumerist, free-market world. Selling their preferred version of a single global marketplace to the public, they portray globalization in a positive light as an indispensable tool for the realization of a better global order.

Such favourable visions of globalization as market integration still shape public opinion and political choices in many parts of the world. Given that the exchange of commodities constitutes one of the core activities of all societies, the market-oriented discourse of globalization itself has turned into an extremely important commodity destined for public consumption. *Business Week*, *The Economist*, *Forbes*, the *Wall Street Journal*, and the *Financial Times* are among the most powerful of dozens of magazines, journals, newspapers, and other electronic media published globally that feed their readers a steady diet of market globalist claims. The constant repetition and public recitation of these slogans have the capacity to produce what they name. As more neoliberal policies are enacted, the claims of market globalism become even more firmly planted in the public mind.

An analysis of hundreds of newspaper and magazine articles— both online and offline—yields five major ideological claims that occur with great regularity in the utterances, speeches, and writings of influential market globalists (see Box 10).

> ## Box 10. The five claims of market globalism
>
> 1. Globalization is about the liberalization and global integration of markets
> 2. Globalization is inevitable and irreversible
> 3. Nobody is in charge of globalization
> 4. Globalization benefits everyone
> 5. Globalization furthers the spread of democracy in the world

Like all ideologies, market globalism starts with the attempt to establish an authoritative definition of its core concept. As we observed in Chapter 3, such an account is anchored in the neoliberal idea of the self-regulating market that serves as the framework for a future global order. But the problem with Claim 1 is that its core message of liberalizing and integrating markets is only realizable through the *political* project of engineering free markets. Thus, market globalists must be prepared to utilize the *powers of government* to weaken and eliminate those social policies and institutions that curtail the market. Since only strong governments are up to this ambitious task of transforming existing social arrangements, the successful liberalization of markets depends upon intervention and *interference* by centralized state power. Such actions, however, stand in stark contrast to the neoliberal idealization of the limited role of government. Yet, market globalists do expect governments to play an extremely active role in implementing their political agenda.

Claim 2 establishes the historical inevitability and irreversibility of globalization understood as the liberalization and global integration of markets. The portrayal of globalization as some sort of natural force, like the weather or gravity, makes it easier for market globalists to convince people that they must adapt to the discipline of the market if they are to survive and prosper. Hence, the claim of inevitability depoliticizes the public discourse about globalization. Neoliberal policies are portrayed to be above politics; they simply carry out what is ordained by nature. As former British Prime Minister Margaret Thatcher put it famously, 'There is no alternative.' If nothing can be done about the 'natural' movement of economic and technological forces, then political resistance would be unnatural, irrational, and dangerous.

Market globalism's deterministic language offers yet another rhetorical advantage. If the natural laws of the market have indeed preordained a neoliberal course of history, then globalization does not reflect the arbitrary agenda of a particular social class or group. In that case, market globalists merely carry out the unalterable imperatives of a benign transcendental force. People aren't in charge of globalization; markets and technology are. But those voices behind Claim 3 are right only in a formal sense. While there is no conscious conspiracy orchestrated by a single, evil force, this does not mean that nobody is in charge of globalization. The liberalization and integration of global markets does not proceed outside the realm of human choice. The market globalist initiative to integrate and deregulate markets around the world both creates and sustains asymmetrical power relations.

Claim 4—globalization benefits everyone—lies at the very core of market globalism because it provides an affirmative answer to the crucial normative question of whether globalization should be considered a 'good' or a 'bad' thing. As we discussed in Chapter 3, market globalists frequently connect their arguments to the alleged benefits resulting from trade liberalization: rising global living standards, economic efficiency, individual freedom, and unprecedented technological progress. But when market dynamics dominate social and political outcomes, the opportunities and rewards of globalization are spread often unequally, concentrating power and wealth amongst a select group of people, regions, and corporations at the expense of the multitude. The same skewed market dynamics also apply to digital access to information (see Figure G).

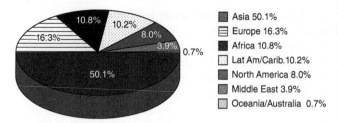

G. Global Internet users in the world by regions, 2019.

Claim 5—globalization furthers the spread of democracy in the world—is rooted in the neoliberal assertion that free markets and democracy are synonymous terms. Persistently affirmed as 'common sense', the actual compatibility of these concepts often goes unchallenged in the public discourse. Indeed, Claim 5 hinges on a conception of democracy that emphasizes formal procedures such as voting at the expense of the direct participation of broad majorities in political and economic decision-making. Hence, the assertion that globalization furthers the spread of democracy in the world is largely based on a rather thin definition of democracy.

Our examination of the five central claims of market globalism suggests that the neoliberal language about globalization is ideological in the sense that it is politically motivated and contributes toward the construction of particular meanings of globalization that preserve and stabilize existing power relations. Market globalism employs powerful narratives that sell an overarching neoliberal worldview, thereby creating collective meanings and shaping people's identities. Over the last two decades, however, massive justice-globalist protests and jihadist-globalist acts of terrorism are clear evidence for the fact that market globalism has encountered ideological resistance.

Justice globalism

Justice globalism refers to the political ideas and values associated with the social alliances and political actors known as the 'global justice movement' (GJM). It emerged in the 1990s as a progressive network of international NGOs and activist groups, defined in Chapter 4 as a 'global civil society'. Dedicated to the establishment of a more equitable relationship between the global North and South, the GJM agitated for the protection of the global environment, fair trade and international labour issues, human rights, and women's issues. As the 20th century drew to a close, the ideological contest between market globalism and its emerging challenger on the political Left erupted in street protests in many cities around the world. At the famous 'Battle of Seattle', for example, tens of thousands of citizens demonstrated against the neoliberal policies of the WTO (see Figure 15).

15. **Police confronting WTO protesters in downtown Seattle, 30 November 1999.**

In the first decade of the 21st century, the forces of justice globalism maintained their political strength. This was evidenced by the emergence of the World Social Forum (WSF), which serves as *the* key ideological site of justice globalism. The WSF was deliberately set up as a 'shadow organization' to the market globalist WEF in Davos, Switzerland. Its annual meetings in the global South draw tens of thousands of delegates from around the world. Just like market globalists who treated the WEF as a platform to project their ideas and claims to a global audience, justice globalists utilized the WSF to publicize their policy demands for a *new global deal* (see Boxes 11 and 12).

In the wake of the 2008 GFC, various 'Occupy' movements around the world became the new face of justice globalism. In the USA,

Box 11. From the WSF Charter of Principles

1. The World Social Forum is an open meeting place for reflective thinking, democratic debate of ideas, formulation of proposals, free exchange of experiences, and interlinking for effective action by groups and movements of civil society that are opposed to neoliberalism and to domination of the world by capital and any form of imperialism and are committed to building a planetary society directed toward fruitful relationships among humankind and between it and the Earth ... 8. The World Social Forum is a plural, diversified, confessional, nongovernmental, and non-party context that, in a decentralized fashion, interrelates organizations and movements engaged in concrete action at levels from the local to the international to build another world ... 13. As a context for interrelations, the World Social Forum seeks to strengthen and create new national and international links among organizations and movement of society that—in both public and private life—will increase the capacity for non-violent social resistance to the process of dehumanization the world is undergoing ...

Box 12. Global New Deal: five demands

1. A global 'Marshall Plan' that includes a blanket forgiveness of all Third World Debt;
2. Levying of the so-called 'Tobin Tax': a tax on international financial transactions that would benefit the global South;
3. Abolition of offshore financial centres that offer tax havens for wealthy individuals and corporations;
4. Implementation of stringent global environmental agreements;
5. Implementation of a more equitable global development agenda.

Occupy Wall Street (OWS) burst onto the political scene in 2011 as part of a global protest movement that drew activists into the world's major cities within months. Inspired by the popular Arab Spring protests in the Middle East and the *Los Indignados* ('the outraged') demonstrations in Spain, Occupy activists expressed outrage at the inequalities of globalization and the irresponsible practices of many financial institutions. Brandishing their slogan 'We are the 99 per cent', Occupy protesters across the world occupied spaces of symbolic importance—such as New York City's Zuccotti Park near Wall Street—and sought to create, in miniature, the kind of egalitarian society they wanted to live in. Rejecting conventional organizational leadership formations, OWS formed decentralized 'General Assemblies' and working groups. However, their efforts to reach decisions through a consensus-based process turned out to be politically ineffective—a major factor in the relatively quick dissipation of the Occupy movement.

Challenging the central claims of market globalism, justice globalists believe that *another world is possible*, as the WSF's principal slogan suggests. Envisioning the construction of a new world order based on a global redistribution of wealth and power, they emphasize the crucial connection between globalization and

> **Box 13. Five central claims of justice globalism**
>
> 1. Neoliberalism produces global crises.
> 2. Market-driven globalization has increased worldwide disparities in wealth and wellbeing.
> 3. Democratic participation is essential in solving global problems.
> 4. Another world is possible and urgently needed.
> 5. People power, not corporate power!

local wellbeing. Justice globalists accuse market globalist elites of pushing neoliberal policies that are leading to greater global inequality, high levels of unemployment, environmental degradation, and the demise of social welfare. Over the last two decades, justice globalists have formulated five central ideological claims in opposition to the 'corporate agenda' of market globalists (see Box 13).

Religious globalisms

As justice globalists organized demonstrations against the IMF and World Bank, Al Qaeda terrorists struck the USA on 11 September 2001. Nearly 3,000 innocent people from many countries perished in less than two hours, including hundreds of heroic NYC police and firefighters trapped in the collapsing towers of the World Trade Center (see Figure 16). In the years following the attacks, it became clear that Islamist extremists were not confining their terrorist activities to the United States. Regional jihadist networks like ISIS, Al Qaeda, Jemaah Islamiya, Boko Haram, Al Shabaab, and Abu Sayyaf regularly targeted civilians and military personnel around the globe.

ISIS and Al Qaeda are two extremely violent Islamic examples of organizations that subscribe to religious globalism. Other religiously inspired visions of a global political community united

16. The burning twin towers of the World Trade Center, 11 September 2001.

by faith have been espoused by fundamentalist Christian groups such as the Army of God and Christian Identity, the Mormon Church, the Falun Gong sect, the Aum Shinrikyo cult, and Chabad, an orthodox Jewish movement with global ambitions. This is not to suggest that *all* religiously inspired articulations of a global community are conservative, reactionary, or violent. A key point about the religious globalisms, however, is that these ideologies aim at global hegemony and demand to be given primacy and superiority over state-based and secular political structures. In some cases, like ISIS or Aum Shinrikyo, they are prepared to use extremely violent means—often couched in terms like a 'cosmic war'—to achieve their end goal.

While jihadist Islamism is today's most spectacular manifestation of religious globalism, it would be a mistake to equate the ideology of ISIS or Al Qaeda with the religion of Islam or even more peaceful strands of 'political Islam' or 'Islamist fundamentalism'.

Rather, the term 'jihadist Islamism' is meant to apply to those extremely violent strains of Islam-influenced ideologies that place a religiously inspired warfare at the heart of their belief. As the recent terrorist activities of ISIS or Boko Haram have shown, jihadist Islamism is the most influential and successful attempt yet to articulate the rising global imaginary into a religious globalism.

Jihadist Islamism is anchored in the core concepts of *umma* (Islamic community of believers) and *jihad* (both armed and unarmed struggle against unbelief purely for the sake of God and his *umma*). Indeed, jihadist globalists understand the *umma* as a single community of believers united in their belief in the one and only God. Expressing a religious-populist yearning for strong leaders who set things right by fighting alien invaders and corrupt Islamic elites, they claim to return power back to the 'Muslim masses' and restore the *umma* to its earlier glory. In their view, the process of regeneration must start with a small but dedicated vanguard of religious warriors willing to sacrifice their lives as martyrs to the holy cause of awakening people to their sacred duties—not just in traditionally Islamic countries, but wherever members of the *umma* yearn for the necessary establishment of God's rule on earth.

With a third of the world's Muslims living today as minorities in non-Islamic countries, jihadist Islamists regard the restoration as no longer a local, national, or even regional event. Rather, it requires a concerted *global* effort spearheaded by jihadists operating in various localities around the world. Indeed, this form of religious globalism holds special appeal for Muslim youths between the ages of 15 and 30 who have lived for sustained periods of time in the individualized and deculturated environments of Westernized Islam. This new wave of jihadist recruits, responsible for some of the most spectacular terrorist operations of the last two decades, were products of a Westernized Islam.

Thus, jihadist globalism takes place in a global space emancipated from the confining territoriality of 'Syria', or the 'Middle East' that used to constitute the political framework of religious nationalists fighting modern secular regimes in the 20th century. Although organizations like ISIS embrace the Manichean dualism of a 'clash of civilizations' between their imagined *umma* and 'global unbelief ', their globalist ideology clearly transcends clear-cut civilizational fault lines. While jihadist Islamism still retains potent metaphors that resonate with people's national or even tribal solidarities, its chilling vision contains an ideological alternative to both market globalism and justice globalism that imagines community in unambiguously global terms.

The challenge of antiglobalist populism

The dire economic consequences of the Global Financial Crisis and the European Sovereign Debt Crisis were amplified by the willingness to support harsh austerity policies that hit ordinary people hard as well as the failure of the neoliberal establishment to punish the financial sector for its economic irresponsibility. In addition, the perceived threat to traditional cultural identities posed by the enhanced migration flows in the mid-2010s caused a profound shift in the ideological landscape away from the neoliberal vision of a globally integrated world. Ordinary people's belief in the claims of market globalism gave way to widespread fears that the great experiment of transcending the nation-state had spiralled out of control and needed to be curbed. Accusing 'cosmopolitan elites' of cheating the toiling masses, authoritarian politicians soon capitalized on this popular discontent by promising 'the forgotten people' a return to national control. Such calls had been issued by various national populist politicians such as Patrick Buchanan in the USA or Joerg Haider in Austria as far back as the 1980s, but had failed to appeal to most voters of conventional mainstream parties.

The full extent of people's anger and resentment toward politics-as-usual was reflected in the unexpected 2016 victory of the pro-Brexit forces in the UK and the stunning election of Donald J. Trump in the United States a few months later. Indeed, the growing power of *right-wing national populism*—and the crucial role played by the digital social media in its meteoric rise—prompted influential media pundits to speak of a *populist explosion* (see Box 14).

But this populist surge did not stop in 2016. Over the last years, national populists have consolidated their gains, most recently in the 2019 European parliamentary elections. Their parties and candidates vaulted to the top spot not only in their previous strongholds of Hungary and Poland, but also in large, traditionally centrist countries such as France and Italy. But the biggest

Box 14. What is national populism?

The French philosopher Jean-Pierre Taguieff coined the term *national populism* in 1984 in reference to the political discourse of Jean-Marie Le Pen and his right-wing French political party, *Front National* ('National Front'), renamed in 2018 under the leadership of his daughter Marine Le Pen as *Rassemblement National* ('National Rally'). National populists imagine a mythical national unity based on an essentialized identity linking ethnicity/race and culture. They claim to defend and protect the pure 'common people' against the treachery of 'corrupt elites' and 'parasitical' political institutions. Privileging a direct relationship between the leader and 'the people', national populists often combine working-class values of the Left with anti-immigrant views of the Right. Over the years, a growing number of populism scholars have adopted 'national populism' as an umbrella term for a range of right-wing variants linked to different geographic regions in the world.

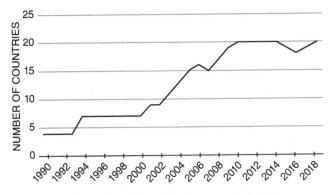

H. Number of countries with populists in power, 1990–2018.

surprise hit the UK where Nigel Farage's newly formed Brexit Party came in first with an astonishing 32 per cent of the vote.

The illiberal and authoritarian leanings of national populism stand in stark contrast to the pluralist and inclusive values of liberal democracy. Yet, populism has been successful in both liberal democracies and authoritarian countries such as Victor Órban's Hungary, Vladimir Putin's Russia, Jair Bolsonaro's Brazil, Norbert Hofer's Austria, Marine Le Pen's France, Matteo Salvini's Italy, Jarosław Kaczyński's Poland, Nigel Farage's United Kingdom, Pauline Hanson's Australia, Iván Duque's Colombia, Rodrigo Duterte's Philippines, and, of course, Donald Trump's United States of America (see Figure H).

Mapping Trump's antiglobalist populism

In order to get a better sense of the ideological make-up of national populism, let us examine 'Trumpism' as an example of a particularly potent strain that originated in the political discourse of American national populists like Patrick Buchanan and Ross Perot in the 1990s. Amplified by Trump's rhetoric, these narratives place pejorative meanings of 'globalization' and 'globalism' at their very conceptual core. An analysis of key speeches given by Donald Trump during his 2016 presidential campaign as well as major public addresses delivered during the first three years of his presidential term (2017–19) reveals his strong antipathy for 'globalism' in favour of *economic nationalism*, the view that the economy should be designed in ways that, first and foremost, serve narrow national interests.

Trumpism employs conventional national populist core concepts such as *the pure people* as holders of the *general will* who struggle against *the corrupt elites*. Accused of undermining the will of the people with the help of the corporate media, these economic, political, and cultural members of the 'establishment' are said to advance their morally corrupt practices of 'selling out the wealth of our nation generated by working people' and filling their own pockets. But Trumpism also links the meaning of 'the elites' to the spectre of 'globalist enemies' working against the interests of the country. While some of these are explicitly identified as domestic actors such as 'Wall Street bankers' or 'Washington politicians', others are characterized as 'foreign agents'. These include both individuals such as George Soros and other members of the 'international financial elite' as well as entire countries like China, Mexico, and Japan, which are denounced for the alleged misdeeds of 'subsidizing their goods', 'devaluing their currencies', 'violating their agreements', and for 'sending rapists, drug dealers, and other criminals into America'.

For this reason, Trump bashes 'globalism' as both a set of 'misguided' public policies and a 'hateful foreign ideology' devised by members of 'the global power structure' who plot 'in secret to destroy America'. Globalists serve the larger material process of 'globalization', defined by Trump as an elite-engineered project of 'abolishing the nation-state' and creating an international system that functions 'to the detriment of the American worker and the American economy'. Finally, Trump associates globalization with what he calls the 'complete and total disasters' of immigration, crime, and terrorism that are 'destroying our nation'. Immigration, in particular, receives ample treatment in the form of vigorous denunciations of the establishment's 'globalist policies of open borders' that are alleged to endanger the safety and security of the American people.

For Trump, the realization of his central campaign slogan to 'make America great again' requires the systematic separation of the 'national' from the 'global' in all aspects of social life in the USA. Warning his audience not to surrender to 'the false song of globalism' Trump emphasizes that 'The nation-state remains the true foundation for happiness and harmony'. The constant repetition of his nationalist mantra—*Americanism, not globalism, will be our credo*—indicates the enormous significance of globalization-related concepts in Trump's political discourse. In this context, it is important to remember that the meaning of 'credo' carries deeply religious connotations that signify the very essence of a belief-system.

For this reason, I refer to this strain of national populism as *antiglobalist populism*. No question, Trump's antiglobalist ideas have produced strong ideological claims that challenge some dominant neoliberal meanings of market globalism (see Box 15).

Ironically, of course, the brand name 'Trump' can hardly be confined to 'Americanism'. Rather it stands for a *global* network of hotels from Honolulu to Rio de Janeiro. His national populist denunciations of globalization notwithstanding, the mounting antiglobalist wave he represents is a globalizing force that has been sweeping across the world. The enduring dynamics of global interconnectivity and global consciousness—inherent even in antiglobalist populism—suggest that globalization continues to provide the overarching conceptual framework and master metanarrative in an age that has increasingly come to doubt the

> **Box 15. Three central claims of Trump's antiglobalist populism**
>
> 1. Corrupt elites betray the hardworking American people by shoring up a global order that makes them rich and powerful while compromising the sovereignty and security of the homeland and squandering the wealth of the nation.
> 2. Americanism, not globalism, will be our credo!
> 3. The defeat of globalism and its treacherous ideologues will usher in a bright future through the glorious rebirth of the nation.

neoliberal programme of worldwide integration. In short, *globalization matters* and continues to serve as a touchstone for vigorous debates on its benefits and possible future trajectories. Let us, then, conclude our discussion with a brief speculation on the future of globalization.

Chapter 8
The future of globalization

As we concluded in Chapter 7, the ideological struggle over the meaning and direction of globalization has shown no signs of dissipating. Still, the current national populist surge has made this epic battle of ideas less over *which* articulation of the global imaginary might prevail and more about *whether* globalism—in any of its competing variations—might be eclipsed by the rebounding national imaginary. Moreover, the uneven intensification of social relations and consciousness across world-space and world-time has both generated and responded to new global problems that are beyond the reach of any single nation-state. Perhaps the three most daunting tasks facing humanity in the 21st century are the *preservation of our wondrous planet*, the *reduction of global inequality*, and the *strengthening of human security*, including in the expanding domain of cyberspace. Will we tackle these global problems in a cooperative, transnational manner or are we on the brink of a new nationalist era of conflict that might halt the powerful momentum of interconnectivity?

In response to this question, let us consider *three possible future scenarios*. The first is predicated upon a further intensification of the current populist *backlash against globalization*. One can think of at least three major social developments resulting from the possible growing strength of antiglobalist sentiments: *further*

restrictions on major forms of mobility; the *decline of*
representative democracy and the rise of illiberal authoritarianism;
and the *failure to build new institutional forms of international*
coordination capable of tackling our mounting global problems.

With regard to the growth of restrictions on major forms of
mobility such as the movement of goods, services, and money, the
current populist surge has already provided us with some early
warning signs. More intense border controls and national security
measures at the world's major airports and seaports have made
international trade more cumbersome. Most importantly,
however, populist leaders like President Trump see global trade as
a zero-sum game between self-interested nations. Thus, they are
prepared to impose steep tariffs on goods and services in order to
reduce their country's trade deficit. If Trump remains in office
beyond 2020, one could easily imagine that what started in 2019
as a trade skirmish between the United States and China could
grow over the next decade into a full-blown trade war that might
draw other countries and regions into its orbit. As a result,
consumers—especially those located in the more prosperous
global North—would not only have to put up with higher prices
for many commodities and services, but also face the likelihood of
the intensifying trade war adversely affecting the health of the
entire world economy.

After all, for all of the inequalities created by unbridled free-
market capitalism, the history of the 20th century teaches us that
trade protectionism often exacerbates a relentless logic of
nationalist competition that rarely remains confined to the
economic sphere. This danger clearly applies in our present era of
multiple national powers, which, once again, compete hard for
honour and influence (see Figure 17). With the world's largest
military arsenal at the command of an unpredictable and
authoritarian populist US president who promised to make his
nation 'great again', any real or perceived threats to America's
economic dominance by publicly identified 'adversaries' like

17. Chinese President Xi Jinping and US President Donald Trump at the G-20 Summit in Japan, 29 June 2019.

China or Iran might turn into a military confrontation that could engulf the whole planet.

The same ominous outlook also holds for enhanced restrictions on transnational movements of people, whether in the form of business travellers, tourists, economic migrants, or political refugees. As demonstrated by drastic populist measures against the transnational flows of political refugees and migrants discussed in Chapter 4, the backlash scenario favours a future characterized by the widespread curtailment of the movement of human bodies in ways that have already compromised the civil liberties of tens of millions of migrants and violated their basic human rights. National populists are especially skilful at exploiting people's legitimate fears of the social and cultural consequences of large numbers of newcomers by branding them as undesirable 'others', unworthy of sustained aid or systematic measures of integration. Open hostility directed at these 'undeserving foreigners', in turn, would further exacerbate the exploitation of existing political divisions and cultural cleavages.

The chaotic unfolding of the Brexit negotiations and the first term of the Trump presidency are instructive examples of the second major social dynamic fuelling the backlash scenario: the weakening of representative democracy and liberal values and the strengthening of political authoritarianism. As the promises of market globalists—especially the central ideological claim that it will benefit everyone—have turned into the reality of runaway inequality and the perceived loss of national traditions and cultural identity, people blame governing elites usually affiliated with established mainstream parties for the dire consequences of what appears to them as 'globalization run amok'. The result is a loss of legitimacy of national governments that seem to be unwilling to protect their citizens from the dizzying speed and tremendous force of social change brought on by globalization.

A third social dynamic fuelling this *backlash scenario* is the loss of momentum in building new global governance structures and transnational institutional networks capable of coordinated action to solve the global problems of our time. Climate change tops the list of these pressing issues. As recent reports have shown, the climatic changes affecting our planet are both real and profound. Debates actively resound through the halls of academe and the seminar rooms of international and non-governmental organizations—though less urgently in the world's parliaments and corporate boardrooms—suggesting that climate change is on a runaway course.

The *second possible future trajectory* of globalization is built on the possibility of massive and enduring losses of antiglobalist populists at the ballot box, thus indicating the cresting of the populist wave and the return of a more globally oriented outlook. Such a *rebound scenario* might start with the electoral defeat of President Trump in 2020 and perhaps the calling of a new Brexit referendum that reverses the 2016 outcome. Given that this trajectory projects the weakening of right-wing *nationalists*—and thus the waning appeal of the national imaginary—it appears unlikely that left-wing *nationalists* would be returned to power. For this reason, let us briefly play out the more likely second option, which could be called *neoliberal globalization with a high-tech face.*

Having been confronted with the populist backlash to the negative consequences of unbridled global market integration, newly empowered market globalists in the 2020s might exert more caution and make some moderate adjustments to their ultimate goal, the creation of a single global free market. Most likely, they would pledge to restore the liberal postwar international order of the past and propose more 'socially responsible' forms of neoliberal globalization to the public. The programmatic outline of such reformed market globalism for the 2020s is already in the making at important ideological sites of global capitalism such as the World Economic Forum (WEF). Built upon claims of the touted benefits of digital globalization, the new vision has been called 'Globalization 4.0' and has been heavily promoted by Klaus Schwab, the German founder and executive chairman of the WEF. Indeed, the official theme of the 2019 WEF Annual Meeting in Davos, Switzerland, was *Globalization 4.0: Shaping the Global Architecture in the Age of the Fourth Industrial Revolution.*

Asserting that the world finds itself today in the throes of a *fourth industrial revolution*—the 'complete digitization of the social, political, and economic'—Schwab predicts a transformation of existing social structures in profound ways that would blur the lines between physical, digital, and biological spheres. Admitting that the free-market consensus of the 1990s and 2000s had been smashed by the populist challenge and was beyond repair, the WEF boss further concedes that, although neoliberal globalization has lifted millions out of poverty in the global South, it has also produced 'eroding incomes' and 'precarious working conditions' for many people in the global North. Populists and protectionists had fed on these ills, but their solutions were misguided attempts to return to a less globalized world that had vanished for good.

The solution is to reform globalization by means of the new leading technologies of the 21st century such as artificial intelligence, autonomous vehicles, quantum computing, 3D printing, and the Internet of Things.

However, there remain serious issues with this rosy future scenario of a new and 'healthier' neoliberal globalization with a high-tech face. These include the widening gap between winners and losers of the Fourth Industrial Revolution, the digitized spread of misinformation through social media, and the increasing reliance on robots and algorithms in all spheres of life. Indeed, many experts warn that digital technology not only creates conveniences, but also eliminates millions of jobs through automation. The combination of neoliberal globalization and robotics might create what economist Richard Baldwin calls a *globotics upheaval* that threatens to disrupt the economy and overwhelm society's capacity to adapt. Harvard business expert Shoshana Zuboff points to another downside of the rebound scenario: the new exploitative capitalist practices of corporate digital giants like Google and Facebook who unilaterally claim human experience as free material for translation into behavioural data designed to fuel and shape consumerist desires towards profitable outcomes (see Box 16).

The *third globalization trajectory*—perhaps the most likely of the three—is based on a possible prolonged *stalemate* between the somewhat weakening national populist forces and the rebounding phalanx of reformist market globalists of Schwab's WEF ilk. Some recent political developments such as the results of the 2018 US mid-term elections and the 2019 European parliamentary elections seem to point to a roughly equal balance of power between centrist parties and the right-wing populists. Another notable trend in the global political arena is the clear upswing of Green parties and the broadening appeal of their environmentalist agenda, which would indicate good news for the currently stagnant fortunes of justice globalism.

Box 16. The dark side of Globalization 4.0: *Surveillance Capitalism*

Surveillance capitalism runs contrary to the early digital dream...Instead, it strips away the illusion that the networked form has some kind of indigenous moral content, that being 'connected' is somehow intrinsically pro-social, innately inclusive, or naturally tending toward the democratization of knowledge. Digital connection is now means to others' commercial ends. At its core, surveillance capitalism is parasitic and self-referential. It revives Karl Marx's old image of capitalism as a vampire that feeds on labor, but with an unexpected turn. Instead of labor, surveillance capitalism feeds on every aspect of the human experience...Google invented and perfected surveillance capitalism...and it quickly spread to Facebook and later Microsoft.

However, a prolonged stalemate between nationalists and globalists would mean that little meaningful progress could be made toward addressing the escalating global problems we discussed in this book. The resulting political gridlock would increase the chances of new global systemic crises rearing their heads in the financial world, cyberspace, the environment, the workplace, and so on—or perhaps a noxious combination of several of these maladies. It is difficult to predict what would happen if another global calamity of the magnitude of the 2008 GFC were to hit the world. The political history of the last two centuries suggests that the reactionary forces of the Right might find themselves at an advantage, because they have proven to be more adroit in using people's fears for their purposes than the Left. The resulting shift to authoritarianism—or, even worse, dictatorship—might spell the end of the era of liberal democracy as we know it. In the face of such alarming crisis situations, it is obvious that the world needs, more than ever, a fundamentally different vision of what our planet could look like. In his hopeful documentary film *2040*, award-winning director Damon Gameau offers an artistic sketch of what the future could look like by the year 2040, if we simply embrace the best solutions already available to us to improve our planet and shift them into the mainstream.

The search for more inclusive and sustainable ways of dealing with global problems must eschew the nationalist reflex to return to an unrecoverable past and instead draw on a more cosmopolitan spirit that calls for the creation of new global institutions and cooperative networks that would be more attuned to the needs of ordinary people around the world. The emergence of the G20 as a sometimes surprisingly effective deliberative body with the ability to design and coordinate action on a global scale suggests that the idea of global governance is perhaps not as utopian today as it was only a quarter-century ago. Other success stories such as the worldwide reduction of absolute poverty and the formation of an international alliance dedicated to the joint exploration of outer space suggest that the solution to our global problems is not less, but more, and better, globalization.

Without question, the years and decades ahead will bring new global crises and further challenges. Humanity has reached yet another critical juncture—the most significant yet in the relatively short existence of our species. Unless we are willing to let global problems fester to the point where violence and intolerance appear to be the only realistic ways of coping with our unevenly integrating societies, we must link the future course of globalization to the creation of a more just and sustainable world. The necessary transformative social processes must be guided by the polestar of an ethical globalism: the building of a truly democratic and egalitarian global order that protects universal human rights, and our planet, without destroying the biological and cultural diversity that is the lifeblood of human evolution.

References and further reading

There is a great deal of academic literature on globalization. But many of these books are not easily accessible to those who want to acquire some basic knowledge of the subject. However, readers who have digested the present volume might find it easier to approach some of the academic works listed here. Some of them have influenced the arguments made in the present volume. Following the overall organization of this book series, however, I have kept direct quotations to a minimum. Still, I wish to acknowledge my intellectual debt to these authors, whose influence on this book is not always obvious from the text.

Chapter 1: What is globalization?

For an insightful discussion of his concept of a 'global systemic shift', see Roland Benedikter, 'Global Systemic Shift: A Multidimensional Approach to Understand the Present Phase of Globalization', *New Global Studies*, vol. 7.1 (2013), pp. 1–15.

A comprehensive elucidation of leading theoretical approaches to understanding globalization can be found in Barrie Axford, *Theories of Globalization* (Polity, 2014).

The data for Box 2 are taken from: <http://www.traveller.com.au/>.

For a better understanding of 'glocalization', consult Roland Robertson, 'Globalisation or Glocalisation?', *The Journal of International Communication*, vol. 18.2 (2012), pp. 191–208; and Victor Roudometof, *Glocalization: A Critical Introduction* (Routledge, 2016).

There are now several excellent academic journals dedicated to the study of globalization such as: *Globalizations*, *Global Networks*, *New Global Studies*, and *Global Perspectives*.

For an introduction to the transdisciplinary field of global studies, see Manfred B. Steger and Amentahru Wahlrab, *What Is Global Studies? Theory & Practice* (Routledge, 2017); Eve Darian-Smith and Philip McCarthy *The Global Turn: Theories, Research Designs, and Methods for Global Studies* (University of California Press, 2017); and Mark Juergensmeyer, Saskia Sassen, and Manfred B. Steger, eds, *The Oxford Handbook of Global Studies* (Oxford University Press, 2019).

Matt Stopera's story of his encounter with 'Brother Orange' can be found in 'I followed My Stolen iPhone Across the World, Became a Celebrity in China, and Found a Friend for Life', <https://www.buzzfeed.com/mjs538/i-followed-my-stolen-iphone-across-the-world-became-a-celebr?utm_source=dynamic&utm_campaign=bfshareemail>.

Additional short articles on this amazing tale of the lost iPhone include: Minh Nguyen, 'The Story of "Brother Orange" is Headed to the Big Screen', <https://www.nbcnews.com/news/asian-america/brother-orange-headed-big-screen-n607446>; NPR Staff, 'Buzzfeed Writer's Stolen Phone Sparks Chinese Viral Sensation', <https://www.npr.org/2015/04/02/397096994/buzzfeed-writers-stolen-phone-sparks-chinese-viral-sensation>; and Taylor Lorenz, 'How a man's stolen iPhone made him an internet celebrity in China', <https://www.businessinsider.com.au/matt-stopera-weibo-celebrity-china-iphone-2015-2>.

For a comprehensive report on recent dynamics involving disembodied globalization, see McKinsey Global Institute (2016), 'Digital Globalization: The New Era of Global Flows'; <https://www.mckinsey.com/business-functions/digital-mckinsey/our-insights/digital-globalization-the-new-era-of-global-flows>.

The parable of the blind scholars and the elephant most likely originated in the Pali Buddhist Udana, a collection of Buddhist stories compiled in the 2nd century BCE. The many versions of the parable spread to other religions as well, especially to Hinduism and Islam. My thanks go to Professor Ramdas Lamb at the University of Hawai'i at Mānoa for sharing his deep understanding of the story.

Chapter 2: Globalization in history

My discussion in the early part of this chapter has greatly benefited from the arguments made by Jared Diamond in his Pulitzer-prize-winning book *Guns, Germs, and Steel* (Norton, 1999). I also recommend a delightful and very readable history of globalization assembled by Nayan Chandra, *Bound Together: How Traders, Preachers, Adventurers, and Warriors Shaped Globalization* (Yale University Press, 2007).

I recommend two accessible books surveying the growing field of global history: Pamela Kyle Crossley, *What is Global History?* (Polity, 2008); and Sebastian Conrad, *What Is Global History?* (Princeton University Press, 2017). Two excellent academic journals on the subject are: *Journal of World History* and *Journal of Global History*.

For a short introduction to the 'world-system theory' approach, see Immanuel Wallerstein, *World-System Analysis: An Introduction* (Duke University Press, 2004).

Chapter 3: The economic dimension of globalization

A creative treatment of economic globalization is provided by Pietra Rivoli, *The Travels of a T-Shirt in the Global Economy*, 2nd edn (Wiley, 2015). The best textbook on the subject is Peter Dicken, *Global Shift: Mapping the Contours of the World Economy*, 7th edn (The Guilford Press, 2015).

An overview of neoliberalism can be found in Manfred B. Steger and Ravi K. Roy, *Neoliberalism: A Very Short Introduction*, 2nd edn (Oxford University Press, 2020).

The 2018 Annual Oxfam Report can be accessed at: <https://resources.oxfam.org.au>.

On the subject of global inequality, see Thomas Piketty, *Capital in the Twenty-First Century* (The Belknap Press, 2014); and Branko Milanovic, *Global Inequality: A New Approach for the Age of Globalization* (The Belknap Press, 2018).

The 2018 Jubilee Debt Campaign report can be accessed at: <https://jubileedebt.org.uk/press-release/developing-country-debt-payments-increase-by-60-in-three-years>.

The best short treatment of the Global Financial Crisis is Robert J. Holton, *Global Finance* (Routledge, 2012).

A comprehensive account of the GFC and the ESDC can be found in Adam Tooze, *Crashed: How a Decade of Financial Crises Changed the World* (Viking, 2018).

Detailed data of the groundbreaking study of TNC networks referred to in this chapter can be found in Stefania Vitali, James B. Glattfelder, and Stefano Battiston, 'The Network of Global Corporate Control', *PLoS* One 6.10 (October 2011), pp. 1–6.

The best sources for empirical data on economic globalization are the annual editions of the UN *Human Development Report* (Oxford University Press), the World Bank's *World Development Report* (Oxford University Press), and the WTO's annual *International Trade Statistics*.

Chapter 4: The political dimension of globalization

The best introduction to political globalization is John Baylis and Steve Smith, *The Globalization of World Politics*, 7th edn (Oxford University Press, 2017).

For the arguments of hyperglobalizers, see Kenichi Ohmae, *The End of the Nation-State* (Free Press, 1995); and Thomas Friedman, *The Lexus and the Olive Tree: Understanding Globalization* (Farrar Straus Giroux, 1999). For the position of the globalization sceptics, see Paul Hirst, Grahame Thompson, and Simon Bromley, *Globalization in Question*, 3rd edn (Polity, 2009).

For the complete Mueller Report from which the excerpt in Box 8 was taken, see Robert S. Mueller III, 'Report on the Investigation into Russian Interference in the 2016 Presidential Election', Washington, DC, March 2019, p. 1; <https://www.justice.gov/storage/report.pdf.>.

Saskia Sassen's important work on territoriality and global cities contains both sceptical and globalist arguments. See, for example, *Territory, Authority, Rights: From Medieval to Global Assemblages* (Princeton University Press, 2008). A fascinating vision of global governance built on transnational city alliances can be found in Benjamin R. Barber, *If Mayors Ruled the World: Dysfunctional Nations, Rising Cities* (Yale University Press, 2013).

For an accessible introduction to global governance issues, see Thomas G. Weiss and Rorden Wilkinson, *Rethinking Global Governance* (Polity, 2019).

For an informed account of the 2013–16 Ebola Crisis in West Africa and beyond, see Richard Preston, *Crisis in the Red Zone: The Story of the Deadliest Ebola Outbreak in History, and of Outbreaks to Come* (Random House, 2019).

David Held's elements of cosmopolitan democracy are taken from Daniele Archibugi and David Held, eds, *Cosmopolitan Democracy* (Polity Press, 1995), pp. 96–120.

Chapter 5: The cultural dimension of globalization

For a comprehensive study on the cultural dimensions of globalization, see Jan Nederveen Pieterse, *Globalization and Culture: Global Melange*, 4th edn (Rowman & Littlefield, 2020).

For the arguments of pessimistic globalizers, see Benjamin Barber, *Consumed* (W. W. Norton and Company, 2007). For the arguments of optimistic globalizers, see Thomas L. Friedman, *The World Is Flat 3.0: A Brief History of the Twenty-First Century* (Picador, 2007). For the arguments of the sceptics, see Arjun Appadurai, *Modernity at Large* (University of Minnesota Press, 1996).

The excerpt of Pope Francis's climate appeal that appears in Box 9 has been taken from *Laudato Si* ('Praise Be to You'), Encyclical Letter issued by Pope Francis I on 24 May 2015.

For the pivotal role of the global media, see Jack Lule, *Globalization and the Media: Global Village of Babel*, 3rd edn (Rowman & Littlefield, 2018).

On English as a global language, see Robert McCrum, *Globish: How the English Language Became the World's Language* (W. W. Norton, 2010).

Chapter 6: The ecological dimension of globalization

An accessible yet remarkably comprehensive book on ecological globalization is Peter Christoff and Robyn Eckersley, *Globalization and the Environment* (Rowman & Littlefield, 2013).

For a concise explanation of the 'Anthropocene' concept, see Erle C. Ellis, *Anthropocene: A Very Short Introduction* (Oxford University Press, 2018).

For a comprehensive yet accessible overview of global climate change issues that also effectively debunks the myths of climate change deniers, see Robert Henson, *A Thinking Person's Guide to Climate Change*, 2nd edn (American Meteorological Society, 2019).

The Intergovernmental Panel on Climate Change (2018), *Global Warming of 1.5°C* report is available at <http://www.ipcc.ch/report/sr15/>.

The 6th edition of the UN Environment Program's *Global Environmental Outlook* (2019) can be found at: <https://www.unenvironment.org/resources/global-environment-outlook-6>.

The full text of Pope Francis's *Laudato Si* can be found at: <http://www.w2.vatican.va/content/francesco/en/encyclicals/documents/papa-francesco_20150524_enciclica-laudato-si.html>.

Chapter 7: Ideological confrontations over globalization

For a more detailed account of the ideological dimensions of globalization, see Manfred B. Steger, *The Rise of the Global Imaginary: Political Ideologies from the French Revolution to the Global War on Terror* (Oxford University Press, 2009); and *Globalisms: Facing the Populist Challenge* (Rowman & Littlefield, 2020).

A readable account of globalization from a market globalist perspective can be found in Jagdish Bhagwati, *In Defense of Globalization* (Oxford University Press, 2007).

The justice-globalist claims and information on the global justice movement in general can be found in: Manfred B. Steger, James Goodman, and Erin K. Wilson, *Justice Globalism: Ideology, Crises, Policy* (Sage, 2013).

Two excellent academic treatments of jihadist globalism and its affiliated movements can be found in: Olivier Roy, *Globalized Islam: The Search for the New Ummah* (Columbia University Press, 2006) and Roel Meijer, *Global Salafism: Islam's New Religious Movement* (Oxford University Press, 2014).

My quotations of Donald Trump's public remarks were taken from two sources: (a) the American Presidency Project website: <http://presidency.ucsb.edu/2016_election.php>, an authoritative archive for the study of presidential speeches; and (b) the Factbase website: <http://factba.se>, a useful online source for the study of Trump's speeches, tweets, and video materials.

Similarly, in their computer-assisted qualitative analysis of seventy-three formal speeches made by Donald Trump during the 2016 electoral campaign, Michele Lamont and her co-authors identify as one of the central features of Trump's discourse its pejorative references to 'globalization'. See Michelle Lamont, Bo Yun Park, and Elena Ayala-Hurtado, 'Trump's Electoral Speeches and his

Appeal to the American White Working Class', *The British Journal of Sociology*, vol. 68.S1 (2017), pp. 153–80.

For a short introduction to populism, see Cas Mudde and Cristobal Rovira Kaltwasser, *Populism: A Very Short Introduction* (Oxford University Press, 2017). For a comprehensive and erudite analysis of the recent populist surge, see Pippa Norris and Ronald Inglehart, *Cultural Backlash: Trump, Brexit, and Authoritarian Populism* (Cambridge University Press, 2019).

For a steady supply of wide-ranging academic articles on the subject, see the journal *Populism* (Brill): <https://brill.com/view/journals/popu/popu-overview.xml>.

For an informed assessment of the dangers to democracy and liberal values posed by populist authoritarianism, see Larry Diamond, *Ill Winds: Saving Democracy from Russian Rage, Chinese Ambition, and American Complacency* (Penguin Press, 2019).

Chapter 8: The future of globalization

For a fascinating examination of the future of digital globalization and automation, see Richard Baldwin, *The Globotics Upheaval: Globalization, Robotics, and the Future of Work* (Oxford University Press, 2019).

On the fascinating topic of 'surveillance capitalism', see Shoshana Zuboff, *The Age of Surveillance Capitalism: The Fight for a Human Future at the New Frontier of Power* (Public Affairs, 2019); and Timothy Ström, *Globalization and Surveillance* (Rowman & Littlefield, 2020).

In addition to Klaus Schwab's 'Globalization 4.0' concept, the perspective of reformist market globalists is concisely articulated in Dani Rodrik, 'Globalization's Wrong Turn and How It Hurt America', *Foreign Affairs*, vol. 98.4 (2019), pp. 26–33.

The excerpt appearing in Box 16 is taken from Shoshana Zuboff, *The Age of Surveillance Capitalism: The Fight for a Human Future at the New Frontier of Power* (Public Affairs, 2019), p. 9.

For a comprehensive assessment of the current backlash against globalization and its possible future consequences, see Manfred B. Steger and Paul James, *Globalization Matters: Engaging the Global in Unsettled Times* (Cambridge University Press, 2019).

Index

COMMUNISM
A Very Short Introduction
Leslie Holmes

The collapse of communism was one of the most defining moments of the twentieth century. At its peak, more than a third of the world's population had lived under communist power. What is communism? Where did the idea come from and what attracted people to it? What is the future for communism? This Very Short Introduction considers these questions and more in the search to explore and understand communism. Explaining the theory behind its ideology, and examining the history and mindset behind its political, economic and social structures, Leslie Holmes examines the highs and lows of communist power and its future in today's world.

Very readable and with its wealth of detail a most valuable reference book.

Gwyn Griffiths, Morning Star

ECONOMICS
A Very Short Introduction
Partha Dasgupta

Economics has the capacity to offer us deep insights into some of the most formidable problems of life, and offer solutions to them too. Combining a global approach with examples from everyday life, Partha Dasgupta describes the lives of two children who live very different lives in different parts of the world: in the Mid-West USA and in Ethiopia. He compares the obstacles facing them, and the processes that shape their lives, their families, and their futures. He shows how economics uncovers these processes, finds explanations for them, and how it forms policies and solutions.

'An excellent introduction . . . presents mathematical and statistical findings in straightforward prose.'

Financial Times

FREE SPEECH
A Very Short Introduction
Nigel Warburton

'I disapprove of what you say, but I will defend to the death your right to say it' This slogan, attributed to Voltaire, is frequently quoted by defenders of free speech. Yet it is rare to find anyone prepared to defend all expression in every circumstance, especially if the views expressed incite violence. So where do the limits lie? What is the real value of free speech? Here, Nigel Warburton offers a concise guide to important questions facing modern society about the value and limits of free speech: Where should a civilized society draw the line? Should we be free to offend other people's religion? Are there good grounds for censoring pornography? Has the Internet changed everything? This Very Short Introduction is a thought-provoking, accessible, and up-to-date examination of the liberal assumption that free speech is worth preserving at any cost.

'The genius of Nigel Warburton's *Free Speech* lies not only in its extraordinary clarity and incisiveness. Just as important is the way Warburton addresses freedom of speech - and attempts to stifle it - as an issue for the 21st century. More than ever, we need this book.'

Denis Dutton, University of Canterbury, New Zealand

www.oup.com/vsi

ORGANIZATIONS
A Very Short Introduction
Mary Jo Hatch

This *Very Short Introductions* addresses all of these questions and considers many more. Mary Jo Hatch introduces the concept of organizations by presenting definitions and ideas drawn from the a variety of subject areas including the physical sciences, economics, sociology, psychology, anthropology, literature, and the visual and performing arts. Drawing on examples from prehistory and everyday life, from the animal kingdom as well as from business, government, and other formal organizations, Hatch provides a lively and thought provoking introduction to the process of organization.

www.oup.com/vsi

FUNDAMENTALISM
A Very Short Introduction
Malise Ruthven

Malise Ruthven tackles the polemic and stereotypes surrounding
this complex phenomenon - one that eludes him today, a
conclusion impossible to ignore since the events in New York on
September 11 2001. But what does 'fundamentalism' really
mean? Since it was coined by American Protestant evangelicals
in the 1920s, the use of the term 'fundamentalist' has expanded to
include a diverse range of radical conservatives and ideological
purists, not all religious. Ruthven investigates fundamentalism's
historical, social, religious, political, and ideological roots, and
tackles the polemic and stereotypes surrounding this complex
phenomenon - one that eludes simple definition, yet urgently
needs to be understood.

'. . . powerful stuff . . . this book is perceptive and important.'

Observer

www.oup.com/vsi

ONLINE CATALOGUE
A Very Short Introduction

Our online catalogue is designed to make it easy to find your ideal Very Short Introduction. View the entire collection by subject area, watch author videos, read sample chapters, and download reading guides.

http://fds.oup.com/www.oup.co.uk/general/vsi/index.html

SOCIAL MEDIA
Very Short Introduction

Join our community
www.oup.com/vsi

- Join us online at the official Very Short Introductions **Facebook** page.
- Access the thoughts and musings of our authors with our online **blog**.
- Sign up for our monthly **e-newsletter** to receive information on all new titles publishing that month.
- Browse the full range of Very Short Introductions online.
- Read **extracts** from the Introductions for free.
- Visit our library of **Reading Guides**. These guides, written by our expert authors will help you to question again, why you think what you think.
- If you are a teacher or lecturer you can order inspection copies quickly and simply via our website.